Toward the Distant Islands

OTHER BOOKS BY HAYDEN CARRUTH

POETRY

The Crow and the Heart (Macmillan, 1959)

The Norfolk Poems of Hayden Carruth (Prairie Press, 1962)

Nothing for Tigers (Macmillan, 1965)

The Clay Hill Anthology (Prairie Press, 1970)

From Snow and Rock, from Chaos (New Directions, 1973)

Brothers, I Loved You All (Horizon Press, 1978)

If You Call This Cry a Song (Countryman Press, 1983)

The Oldest Killed Lake in North America (Salt-Works Press, 1985)

Asphalt Georgics (New Directions, 1985)

The Selected Poetry of Hayden Carruth (Collier Books, 1985)

Tell Me Again How the White Heron Rises and Flies Across the Nacreous River at Twilight Toward the Distant Islands (New Directions, 1989)

The Sleeping Beauty (Copper Canyon Press, 1990)

Collected Shorter Poems, 1946–1991 (Copper Canyon Press, 1992)

Collected Longer Poems (Copper Canyon Press, 1994)

Scrambled Eggs & Whiskey: Poems, 1991–1995 (Copper Canyon Press, 1996)

Doctor Jazz (Copper Canyon Press, 2001)

PROSE

Effluences from the Sacred Caves (University of Michigan Press, 1983)

Suicides and Jazzers (University of Michigan Press, 1992)

Sitting In: Selected Writings on Jazz, Blues, and Related Topics (University of Iowa Press, 1993)

Selected Essays & Reviews (Copper Canyon Press, 1996)

Reluctantly: Autobiographical Essays (Copper Canyon Press, 1998)

Beside the Shadblow Tree: A Memoir of James Laughlin (Copper Canyon Press, 1999)

HAYDEN CARRUTH

Toward the Distant Islands

NEW & SELECTED POEMS

Edited and with an Introduction by Sam Hamill

COPPER CANYON PRESS

Printed in the United States of America

Cover art: Frank Boyden, *Crowning*, 2002, Ed. 10
Line etching, spitbite, sugarlift on paper, 4 1/2" x 20 1/16"
Collection of the Hallie Ford Museum of Art, Willamette University, Salem,
Oregon, gift of the artist in honor of Maribeth Collins.

Copper Canyon Press is in residence at Fort Worden State Park in
Port Townsend, Washington, under the auspices of Centrum
Foundation. Centrum is a gathering place for artists and creative
thinkers from around the world, students of all ages and backgrounds,
and audiences seeking extraordinary cultural enrichment.

LIBRARY OF CONGRESS CATALOGING-IN-PUBLICATION DATA
Carruth, Hayden, 1921–
  Toward the distant islands / Hayden Carruth; edited and with an
  introduction by Sam Hamill.
      p. cm.
  ISBN 1-55659-236-1 (pbk. : alk. paper)
  I. Hamill, Sam. II. Title.
  PS3505.A77594T69 2006
  811'.54—dc22

                                        2005028705

98765432 FIRST PRINTING

COPPER CANYON PRESS
Post Office Box 271
Port Townsend, Washington 98368
www.coppercanyonpress.org

Contents

New Poems (2001–2005)

Introduction

HAYDEN CARRUTH has wrestled with daemons and angels alike, not least of all himself, in his long writing life. And every rural New England poet—especially of Carruth's generation—must wrestle with the shadows of Henry Thoreau (whose very name most people mispronounce and whose influence very few have condemned) and Robert Frost. In rejecting Thoreau's romantic-transcendentalist view of "nature," Carruth has written of him and of his ideas harshly and often. His essay "The Man in the Box at Walden" is justly famous. If his views of Frost have been kindlier, he has made it nonetheless abundantly clear in all of his work that he is very much his own man, breaking his own ground. Like the jazz he so loves, his poetry ranges from the formal to the spontaneous, from local vernacular to righteous oratory, from beautiful complexity to elegant understatement. His poetry is alive with rare courage and clear-eyed conviction.

Long ago, Carruth wrote,

> I had always been aware that the Universe is sad; everything in it, animate or inanimate, the wild creatures, the stones, the stars, was enveloped in the great sadness, pervaded by it. Existence had no use. It was without end or reason. The most

beautiful things in it, a flower or a song, as well as the most compelling, a desire or a thought, were pointless. So great a sorrow. And I knew that the only rest from my anxiety—for I had been trembling even in infancy—lay in acknowledging and absorbing this sadness… Never then or now have I been able to look at a cloudless sky at night and see beauty there…

The poet's own sadness is reflected in everything he sees, but poetry will transform such a pathetic fallacy in the hands of a good maker. More often, Carruth's "great sorrow" bears a striking resemblance to what the Japanese call *mono-no-ware*— the beautiful sadness of temporality. And when he speaks of trembling, he speaks literally. He has struggled his entire life with severe chronic depression that at one time left him so debilitated and dysfunctional that he was institutionalized and psychiatrists told him he could never live a normal life. He certainly has lived no normal life. He writes eloquently and disturbingly of his attempted suicide and self-destructive behavior. He has written of his "marriage to the bottle." His writes astonishing poems of nature, of love and terrible loss, and writes of aging with eroticism, humor, and terror.

He has stripped himself bare as he has constantly resurrected himself—often with the aid, both financial and psychological, of strong women, loyal friends, and a good doctor (of whom he has written). But his "shamelessness" is not in the tradition of "confessional" poetry; rather it is the result of unblinking and sometimes scarily honest encounters with himself. He sometimes bears a greater resemblance to the great poets of classical Greece or China than to his contemporaries as he assays his world and his place in it, speaking now in the most intimate voice and then in a public one. And yet he insists, "Poetry is not special. It's ordinary. Like music."

He achieved a kind of admirable ordinariness among his neighbors in northern Vermont, where he lived for many years while making a place for himself simultaneously among the literati. He served as editor at *Poetry* magazine, poetry editor for *Harper's*, and for twenty years advisory editor for *The Hudson Review*. He has been husband, father, laborer, rustic bard, lover, existential philosopher (he wrote a book-length imaginary dialogue with Albert Camus), essayist, professor, jazz aficionado, and both official and unofficial editor to several generations of poets. He was fifty-seven years old before he first read his poetry in public. This poet, so famous for his years of poverty and isolation, has in fact been in constant communion with the world—both the physical world of his hardscrabble life and the intellectual world that quickly transcends boundaries and generations.

In his introduction to *Effluences from the Sacred Caves* (essays and reviews, University of Michigan Press, 1983), Carruth writes,

> I can define myself—to the extent possible at all—only *against* [his emphasis] the Platonic and Romantic aspirations that still hold out to me a powerful, though I think false, allure.
>
> ...I was raised a radical agnostic and relativist.

. . . And so I caught the transcending fever, and I
sought ways to rise above the objective ego and
become a self in pure subjectivity, free and undeter-
mined, an authentic existential independency. Yet
at the same time my back-country hardheadedness
made me vehemently disclaim any Transcen-
dentalism in my transcension, and made me equal-
ly aware of the need for responsibility not only to
the self but to others. I saw how in its moments of
transcendent freedom the self is, in fact, a com-
munion with the other, though how to define that
other still escapes me. I think it may be the tran-
scendent selves of all human imaginations not
irreparably maimed by the life of machines in the
objective world. I call it love.

Sustained by this love, by communion, by an abiding sense
of responsibility, he has written two dozen volumes of superb
poetry and several volumes of essays, autobiographical writings,
and reviews. He has been one of the most rigorous and inventive
technicians of a generation that will be long celebrated for its
brilliance and variety. Whether writing in the vernacular of jazz
or in the traditions of the sonnet; whether reinventing the haiku,
inventing new forms, or mastering idiomatic "open" forms;
whether in lyric or narrative modes, his has been a unique,
autochthonous voice—transcendental in the singing itself.

In his Foreword to Carruth's 1985 *Selected Poetry* (Collier
Books), Galway Kinnell wrote, "Technically, he is a virtuoso. He
writes subtle, finely tuned poems in rhyme and meter; syllabics;

and in highly formalized free verse. He also writes free verse so invisibly artful that under its spell we are not in the presence of a poem, but of the world." Indeed, just as there is a "world of Yeats" or a world of Dickinson or Whitman or Rexroth, Carruth's great body of work is a world. A wise reader might want to read his essays on jazz, for instance, while reading *The Sleeping Beauty*—and listen to the music as worlds unfold. And behind that, of course, is his lifetime of concentrated listening—not only to the jazz he writes about but also to the vernacular of his neighbors in northern Vermont, to birdsong and nightsound. Writing poetry is a form of concentrated listening.

This is a body of work that has been made—to use Ezra Pound's famous phrase—to endure, to live with. How does one *edit* a world? I have chosen not to excerpt fragments or sections from the poet's longer poems. While doing so might serve as an introduction to the reader, I believe it is, ultimately, a profound disservice to the poetry—and in the longer view, probably a disservice to the reader as well, depriving one of the pleasure of experiencing the unfolding of each poem in its proper context. His "Paragraphs," for instance, are an invented form, are sequential, and should be experienced as such.

While rereading Carruth's oeuvre, I held in mind two objectives: to provide a good introductory sampling from his shorter poems, hoping the uninitiated reader would be enticed into exploring the larger body of work; and to produce a worthy "portable Carruth," a little celebration of "greatest hits" including some recent and previously unpublished work, something considerably less than half the size of his *Collected Shorter Poems*.

While one must ultimately turn to the full body of published work to appreciate the sweep of his vision, a portable Carruth is a useful tool.

In my endeavors, I have benefited greatly from the counsel of the poet and his wife (and fellow poet), Joe-Anne McLaughlin. They also join me in thanking Art Hanlon for his generous and diligent work in preparing the manuscript.

Writing of himself in the third person in "Fragments of Autobiography: Second Series," (1998) the poet says, "For Carruth the most beautiful thing on earth was not the earth: it was the starry sky at night... brilliant stars in their millions..." His devotion to poetry has sustained him through the long arduous decades of struggle, and through his practice he has realized transcendence in the poetry itself.

SAM HAMILL
Kage-an, 2005

FROM *The Crow and the Heart* (1959)

The Buddhist Painter Prepares to Paint

First he must go where
Not even the birds will brave his solitude,
Alone to the sunburnt plain to try his mood
    In silence. Prayer

Will help him to begin
Perhaps, or tell him if after all tomorrow
May not be better. But, alas, his sorrow
    Is genuine,

The requisite of art.
He kneels, eyes bent in humble palms. To see
In perfect light is difficult; one must be
    Blind from the start.

And then the sevenfold
Office, the chanting of the hundred names,
The offering of flowers, none the sun shames,
    But marigold

Of his imagination,
Jasmine of the pure mind, ghostly for the ghost
Of Buddha; he speaks the uttermost
    Foliation,

He whispers, he merely thinks,
Thinking the perfect flower of the universe.
And the primal vastness comes to intersperse
    His thoughts, he sinks

Through the four phases
Of infinity to the abyss, crying, "Die,
O world. Sunburnt grasses, fade." The sky
    Turns on its huge axis

    Under him; all is lost,
Fingers, heartbeat, the singing brain, gone,
Or glittering there in that resplendent one
    Who shimmers, posed

    In the wide abyss.
The holy impassivity of his goddess dances
Without motion. The painter sighs. Expanses
    Of unknown bliss

    Widen through death, through birth,
Acheless, moving the goddess, the one, the all,
Who dances in the void of the painter's soul.
    But something of earth,

    Something of his old dolor,
Calls back the painter now from the reflected
Essence to the form of the goddess projected
    In line and color.

    His sadness is like the itch
That gives his fingers back: among the many
Loves that preceded his pure ceremony
    There is one which

Denies the formless, paints
Something that might be the goddess dancing, dressed
In green flesh with four arms and three heads, lest
    The loveless saints

    Alone find rapture. Why
Must the painter paint? For love of forms so trite?
Or is it that love of minds and hearts finds sight
    Within his eye?

    The painter's love is his
Great penalty, because to fashion even
This sham goddess, he must deny the heaven
    Where the goddess is.

Reflexive

Of all disquiets sorrow is most serene.
Its intervals of soft humility
Are lenient; they intrude on our obscene
Debasements and our fury like a plea
For wisdom—guilt is always shared. The fears
Fall, if for just an hour, all away,
And the old, essential person reappears.
Sorrow can shape us better than dismay.

You have forgiven me, old friends and lovers,
I think you have forgiven me at last,
As you put by the banished fugitive.
And if I'm sorry who was once aghast
For all the hurts I've done you, I forgive,
I too, the self this sorrow still recovers.

November: Indian Summer

The huge frostbank of the North
Leans over these few days.
Sunlight crumbles in haze,
Saffron of smell and color.
And the chickadees hold forth,
Thick in the ruined quince,
Scolding our complex dolor,
Talkative though long since
We came to a solemn season.
Close your eyes. The warmth
Of sun and the chickadee song
Will take you, against all reason,
To another time on the earth
That was idle and August-long,
When katydids twanged the skies
In peace, months past and more,
Far in your thoughts, as far,
Perhaps, if you close your eyes,
As the summer before the war.

FROM *The Norfolk Poems of Hayden Carruth* (1962)

Purana, Meaning Once Upon a Time

Only the gods may act with perfect impudence—
That is, irrationally. Listen while I retell
A story from a book as old as the Tobey Woods.

It fell on an autumn night, when the forest leaves
Moved like small rustling animals over the moss
And Jumna flowed with a sure deep-running strength,

That Sri Krishna played his flute by the riverbank
And the moonlight dripped like rain from tangled trees.
The music of love came liquidly to the village

Where gopis, who were the milkmaids, drank willlessly,
Their souls tipped to the song in unimagined thirst;
And soon they ran unresistingly to the forest,

One by one, and in groups, tripping and hurrying,
Leaving parents, brothers, sisters, husbands behind,
Leaving their babies whimpering in the cradles.

They said: "Ah, heavily love-laden we will give all."
Conceive the bewilderment in their eyes when Krishna,
Surrounded, the good looks of him bruising the girls,

Rebuked them, saying: "What! Have you come in the night?
Through the forest? Then you care nothing for tigers?
Shame! Respectable girls running after a lover

In the night, sacrificing your lords and your parents,
Your brothers and sisters and children. Pretty girls,
Go back to your places, go back and be content."

Tears melted their eyes and their hearts were frightened;
They looked miserably at one another in their confusion,
And began to scratch the ground with their feet like deer.

At last they said: "Truly we must attend our husbands
And our parents and children, but O Sweet Lord,
When thou art husband, parent, and child is it not just

That we seek the pleasures of all of these in Thee?"
The All-One turned away and I think said nothing,
And sorely, wearily the milkmaids returned to the village,

Their question unanswered. The singing hermit thrush
In Tobey Woods has brought this to my mind.
The leaves are beginning to fall. Soon he will be gone.

Naming for Love

These are the proper names:
Limestone, tufa, coral rag,
Clint, beer stone, braystone,
Porphyry, gneiss, rhyolite,
Ironstone, cairngorm, circle stone,
Blue stone, chalk, box stone,
Sarsen, magnesia, brownstone,
Flint, aventurnine,
Soapstone, alabaster, basalt,
Slate, quartzite, ashlar,
Clunch, cob, gault, grit,
Buhrstone, dolomite,
Flagstone, freestone, sandstone,
Marble, shale, gabbro, clay,
Adamant, gravel, traprock,
And of course brimstone.

Some of the names are shapes:
Crag, scarp, moraine, esker,
Alp, hogback, ledge, tor,
Cliff, boulder, crater,
Gorge, and bedrock.

Some denote uses:
Keystone, capstone,
Hearthstone, whetstone,
And gravestone.

For women a painful stone called
Wombstone, which doctors say is
"A calculus formed in the uterus."
Gallstone and kidneystone hurt everyone.
Millstone is our blessing.

I will not say the names
Of the misnamed precious stones.

But a lovely name is gold,
A product of stone.

Underwards is magma;
May all who read this live long.

Adolf Eichmann

I want no tricks in speaking of this man.
My friends deplore my metaphysical mind,
But now I am a plain and plain-spoken man.

In my life only two men have turned my mind
To vengefulness, and one was this man's chief,
Who was, I now think, probably out of his mind.

But this one is rational. Naturally a mad chief
Needs sane lieutenants. Both were named Adolf,
An ugly Teutonic word which means the chief,

And earlier, in the cold north forest, this Adolf
Meant the wolf, a favorite totem. Let disgrace,
I say, fall for all time to come upon Adolf,

And let no child hereafter bear the disgrace
Of that dirty name. Sometimes in my bed
I study my feet, noticing their disgrace,

For the human foot is an ugly thing. But my bed
Is nothing like the bed that I have seen
Where hundreds of unclothed bodies lay. That bed

Was for dead people, deeply dug, and whoever has seen
Their feet knows the real ugliness and in their voice
Has heard the only true language. I have seen

And I have heard, but my feet live and my voice
Is beautiful and strong, and I say let the dung
Be heaped on that man until it chokes his voice,

Let him be made leprous so that the dung
May snuggle to his bone, let his eyes be shut
With slow blinding, let him be fed his own dung,

But let his ears never, never be shut,
And let young voices read to him, name by name,
From the rolls of all those people whom he has shut

Into the horrible beds, and let his name
Forever and ever be the word for hate,
Eichmann, cast out of the race, a loathsome name

For another kind, a sport spawned in hate
That can never be joined, never, in the world of man.
Lord, forgive me, I can't keep down my hate.

FROM *Nothing for Tigers* (1965)

Burning Dawn

This day lies under glass,
A relic. Blear and wan,
Two feet wade up the dawn,
Tread and fall back like fish,
Two fish as blind as bone.
The sun, the sun beats down.
A vitreous, brittle sky
Expands to the breaking point
Like burnt glass being blown,
And the blind feet go on.
Nothing can keep it now,
This sky that splits apart,
For the cygnet and the swan
On striding wings have flown
Over the shallow hill,
Dripping across the lawn
Droplets of breaking laughter
Like that of the soulless girl
Who was here and has gone.

Freedom and Discipline

Saint Harmony, many
years I have stript

naked in your service
under the lash. Yes,

I believe the first
I heard (living, there

aloud in the hall) was
Sergei Rachmaninoff

set at the keys like a
great dwarf, a barrel

on three spindles,
megalocephalus, hands

with fourteen fingers,
ugly as Merlin, with whom

I was in love, a boy and
an old man; a boy nodding

and an old man sorrowing
under the bushfire of the

people's heart, until he
coolly knocked out the

Prelude in C# Minor. Second
was Coleman Hawkins

in about 1934 perhaps.
I, stript and bleeding,

leapt to the new touch,
up and over the diminished

in a full-voiced authority
of blue-gold blues. I

would do nothing, locked
in discipline, sworn to

freedom. The years shrieked
and smothered, like billboards

beside a road at night.
I learnt how Catlett

drove the beat without
harming it, how Young

sped between the notes,
how Monk reconstructed

a broken chord to make
my knuckles rattle, and much

from oblivion: Newton,
Fasola, Berigan, my

inconsolable Papa Yancey.
Why I went to verse-making

is unknowable, this
grubbing art. Trying,

Harmony, to fix your beat
in things that have none

and want none—absurdity!
Let that be the answer

to any hope of statecraft.
As Yeats said, *Fol de rol.*

Freedom and discipline concur
only in ecstasy, all else

is shoveling out the muck.
Give me my old hot horn.

FROM *The Clay Hill Anthology* (1970)

SELECTED HAIKU

Fathers die, but sons
catch the grave chill, looking in
at lost forgiveness.

*   *   *

The Sanskrit root word
for "war" means literally
"desire for more cows."

*   *   *

Ducks, waking at sea
on greasy billows, taste life
in the fog and brine.

*   *   *

Niobe, your tears
are your children now. See how
we have multiplied.

*   *   *

Why speak of the use
of poetry? Poetry
is what uses us.

*   *   *

One ant turns backward
along the file. The others
pause and hurry past.

*   *   *

Always this special
secret feeling, the failure
of reality.

*   *   *

True, I happen. So
put "I" in. But randomly,
I am not the song.

*   *   *

Let my snow-tracks lead
on, on. Let them, where they stop,
stop. There, in mid-field.

FROM *From Snow and Rock,*
from Chaos (1973)

Concerning Necessity

It's quite true we live
in a kind of rural twilight
most of the time giving
our love to the hard dirt
the water and the weeds
and the difficult woods

ho we say drive the wedge
heave the axe run the hand shovel
dig the potato patch
dig ashes dig gravel
tickle the dyspeptic chainsaw
make him snarl once more

while the henhouse needs cleaning
the fruitless corn to be cut
and the house is falling to pieces
the car coming apart
the boy sitting and complaining
about something everything anything

this was the world foreknown
though I had thought somehow
probably in the delusion
of that idiot Thoreau
that necessity could be saved
by the facts we actually have

like our extreme white birch
clasped in the hemlock's arms
or our baybreasted nuthatch
or our mountain and our stars
and really these things do serve
a little though not enough

what saves the undoubted collapse
of the driven day and the year
is my coming all at once
when she is done in or footsore
or down asleep in the field
or telling a song to a child

coming and seeing her move
in some particular way
that makes me to fall in love
all over with human beauty
the beauty I can't believe
right here where I live.

The Ravine

Stones, brown tufted grass, but no water,
it is dry to the bottom. A seedy eye
of orange hawkweed blinks in sunlight
stupidly, a mink bumbles away,
a ringnecked snake among stones lifts its head
like a spark, a dead young woodcock—
long dead, the mink will not touch it—
sprawls in the hatchment of its soft plumage
and clutches emptiness with drawn talons.
This is the ravine today. But in spring it
cascaded, in winter it filled with snow
until it lay hidden completely. In time,
geologic time, it will melt away
or deepen beyond recognition, a huge
gorge. These are what I remember and foresee.
These are what I see here every day,
not things but relationships of things,
quick changes and slow. These are my sorrow,
for unlike my bright admonitory friends
I see relationships, I do not see things.
These, such as they are, every day, every
unique day, the first in time and the last,
are my thoughts, the sequences of my mind.
I wonder what they mean. Every day,
day after day, I wonder what they mean.

Once More

Once more by the brook the alder leaves
turn mauve, bronze, violet, beautiful
after the green of crude summer; galled
black stems, pithy, tangled, twist in the
flesh-colored vines of wild cyclamen.
Mist drifts below the mountaintop
in prismatic tatters. The brook is full,
spilling down heavily, loudly, in silver
spate from the beaver ponds in the high
marshy meadows. The year is sinking:
heavily, loudly, beautifully. Deer move
heavily in the brush like bears, half drunk
on masty acorns and rotten wild apples.
The pileated woodpecker thumps a dead elm
slowly, irregularly, meditatively.
Like a broken telephone a cricket rings
without assertion in dead asters and
goldenrod; asters gone cloudy with seed,
goldenrod burnt and blackened. A gray trout
rests under the lip of glacial stone. One
by one the alder leaves plunge down to earth,
veering, and lie there, glowing, like a shirt
of Nessus. My heart in my ribs does what it
has done occasionally all my life: thumps and
heaves suddenly in irregular rhythm that makes
me gasp. How many times has this season turned
and gone down? How many! I move heavily

into the bracken, and the deer stand still
a moment, uncertain, before they break away,
snorting and bounding heavily before me.

The Cows at Night

The moon was like a full cup tonight,
too heavy, and sank in the mist
soon after dark, leaving for light

faint stars and the silver leaves
of milkweed beside the road,
gleaming before my car.

Yet I like driving at night
in summer and in Vermont:
the brown road through the mist

of mountain-dark, among farms
so quiet, and the roadside willows
opening out where I saw

the cows. Always a shock
to remember them there, those
great breathings close in the dark.

I stopped, and took my flashlight
to the pasture fence. They turned
to me where they lay, sad

and beautiful faces in the dark,
and I counted them—forty
near and far in the pasture,

turning to me, sad and beautiful
like girls very long ago
who were innocent, and sad

because they were innocent,
and beautiful because they were
sad. I switched off my light.

But I did not want to go,
not yet, nor knew what to do
if I should stay, for how

in that great darkness could I explain
anything, anything at all.
I stood by the fence. And then

very gently it began to rain.

Emergency Haying

Coming home with the last load I ride standing
on the wagon tongue, behind the tractor
in hot exhaust, lank with sweat,

my arms strung
awkwardly along the hayrack, cruciform.
Almost 500 bales we've put up

this afternoon, Marshall and I.
And of course I think of another who hung
like this on another cross. My hands are torn

by baling twine, not nails, and my side is pierced
by my ulcer, not a lance. The acid in my throat
is only hayseed. Yet exhaustion and the way

my body hangs from twisted shoulders, suspended
on two points of pain in the rising
monoxide, recall that greater suffering.

Well, I change grip and the image
fades. It's been an unlucky summer. Heavy rains
brought on the grass tremendously, a monster crop,

but wet, always wet. Haying was long delayed.
Now is our last chance to bring in
the winter's feed, and Marshall needs help.

We mow, rake, bale, and draw the bales
to the barn, these late, half-green,
improperly cured bales; some weigh 150 pounds

or more, yet must be lugged by the twine
across the field, tossed on the load, and then
at the barn unloaded on the conveyor

and distributed in the loft. I help—
I, the desk-servant, word-worker—
and hold up my end pretty well too; but God,

the close of day, how I fall down then. My hands
are sore, they flinch when I light my pipe.
I think of those who have done slave labor,

less able and less well prepared than I.
Rose Marie in the rye fields of Saxony,
her father in the camps of Moldavia

and the Crimea, all clerks and housekeepers
herded to the gaunt fields of torture. Hands
too bloodied cannot bear

even the touch of air, even
the touch of love. I have a friend
whose grandmother cut cane with a machete

and cut and cut, until one day
she snicked her hand off and took it
and threw it grandly at the sky. Now

———

in September our New England mountains
under a clear sky for which we're thankful at last
begin to glow, maples, beeches, birches

in their first color. I look
beyond our famous hayfields to our famous hills,
to the notch where the sunset is beginning,

then in the other direction, eastward,
where a full new-risen moon like a pale
medallion hangs in a lavender cloud

beyond the barn. My eyes
sting with sweat and loveliness. And who
is the Christ now, who

if not I? It must be so. My strength
is legion. And I stand up high
on the wagon tongue in my whole bones to say

woe to you, watch out
you sons of bitches who would drive men and women
to the fields where they can only die.

The Birds of Vietnam

O bright, O swift and bright,
you flashing among pandanus boughs
    (is that right? pandanus?)
under the great banyan, in and out
the dusky delicate bamboo groves
    (yes? banyan, bamboo?)
low, wide-winged, gliding
over the wetlands and drylands
    (but I have not seen you,
    I do not know your names,
    I do not know
    what I am talking about).

I have seen the road runner and the golden eagle,
the great white heron and the Kirtland's warbler,
    our own endangered species,
and I have worried about them. I have worried
about all our own, seen and unseen,
whooping cranes, condors, white-tailed kites,
and the ivory-bills (certainly gone, all gone!)
the ones we have harried, murdered, driven away
as if we were the Appointed Avengers,
    the Destroyers, the Wrathful Ones
out of our ancestors' offended hearts
at the cruel beginning of the world.
But for what? for whom? why?
    Nobody knows.

And why, in my image of that cindered country,
should I waste my mourning? I will never have
enough. Think of the children there,
insane little crusted kids at the beckoning fire,
think of the older ones, burned, crazy with fear,
sensible beings who can know hell, think
of their minds exploding, their hearts flaming.

I do think. But today,
O mindless, O heartless, in and out
the dusky delicate groves,
your hell becomes mine, simply
and without thought, you maimed, you
poisoned in your nests, starved
in the withered forests.
    O mindless, heartless,
      you never invented hell.
We say flesh turns to dust, though more often
a man-corpse or woman-corpse is a bloody pulp,
and a bird-corpse too, yet your feathers
      retain life's color
long afterward, even in the robes
      of barbarous kings,
still golden the trogon feather,
still bright the egret plume, and the crest
of the bower bird will endure forever
almost. You will always remind us of what
      the earth has been.

O bright, swift, gleaming
in dusky groves,
I mourn you.
O mindless, heartless, I can't
help it, I have so loved
        this world.

Abandoned Ranch, Big Bend

Three people come where no people belong any more.
They are a woman who would be young
And good-looking if these now seemed
Real qualities, a child with yellow hair, a man
Hardened in desperate humanity. But here are only
Dry cistern, adobe flaking, a lizard. And now this
Disagreeable feeling that they were summoned. Sun
On the corrugated roof is a horse treading,
A horse with wide wings and heavy hoofs. The lizard
Is splayed head down on the wall, pulsing. They do not
Bother to lift their binoculars to the shimmering distance.
From this dead center the desert spirals away,
Traveling outward and inward, pulsing. Summoned
From half across the world, from snow and rock,
From chaos, they arrived a moment ago, they thought,
In perfect fortuity. There is a presence emerging here in
Sun dance and clicking metal, where the lizard blinks
With eyes whetted for extinction; then swirling
Outward again, outward and upward through the sky's
White-hot funnel. Again and again among the dry
Wailing voices of displaced Yankee ghosts
This ranch is abandoned to terror and the sublime.
The man turns to the woman and child. He has never
Said what he meant. They give him
The steady cool mercy of their unreproachful eyes.

FROM *Brothers, I Loved You All* (1978)

The Loon on Forrester's Pond

Summer wilderness, a blue light
twinkling in trees and water, but even
wilderness is deprived now. "What's that?
What is that sound?" Then it came to me,
this insane song, wavering music
like the cry of the genie inside the lamp,
it came from inside the long wilderness
of my life, a loon's song, and there he was
swimming on the pond, guarding
his mate's nest by the shore,
diving and staying under
unbelievable minutes and coming up
where no one was looking. My friend
told how once in his boyhood
he had seen a loon swimming beneath his boat,
a shape dark and powerful
down in that silent mysterious world, and how
it had ejected a plume of white excrement
curving behind. "It was beautiful,"
he said.

The loon
broke the stillness over the water
again and again,
broke the wilderness
with his song, truly
a vestige, the laugh that transcends

first all mirth
and then all sorrow
and finally all knowledge, dying
into the gentlest quavering timeless
woe. It seemed
the real and only sanity to me.

August First

Late night on the porch, thinking
of old poems. Another day's
work, another evening's,
done. A large moth, probably
Catocala, batters the screen,
but lazily, its strength spent,
its wings tattered. It perches
trembling on the sill. The sky
is hot dark summer, neither
moon nor stars, air unstirring,
darkness complete; and the brook
sounds low, a discourse fumbling
among obstinate stones. I
remember a poem I wrote
years ago when my wife and
I had been married twenty-
two days, an exuberant
poem of love, death, the white
snow, personal purity. Now
I look without seeing at
a geranium on the sill;
and, still full of day and evening,
of what to do for money,
I wonder what became of
purity. The world is a
complex fatigue. The moth tries
once more, wavering desperately

up the screen, beating, insane,
behind the geranium. It
is an immense geranium,
the biggest I've ever seen,
with a stem like a small tree
branching, so that two thick arms
rise against the blackness of
this summer sky, and hold up
ten blossom clusters, bright bursts
of color. What is it—coral,
mallow? Isn't there a color
called "geranium"? No matter.
They are clusters of richness
held against the night in quiet
exultation, five on each branch,
upraised. I bought it myself
and gave it to my young wife
years ago, a plastic cup
with a 19¢ seedling
from the supermarket, now
so thick, leathery-stemmed,
and bountiful with blossom.
The moth rests again, clinging.
The brook talks. The night listens.

Essay

So many poems about the deaths of animals.
Wilbur's toad, Kinnell's porcupine, Eberhart's squirrel,
and that poem by someone—Hecht? Merrill?—
about cremating a woodchuck. But mostly
I remember the outrageous number of them,
as if *every* poet, I too, had written at least
one animal elegy; with the result that today
when I came to a good enough poem by Edwin Brock
about finding a dead fox at the edge of the sea
I could not respond; as if permanent shock
had deadened me. And then after a moment
I began to give way to sorrow (watching myself
sorrowlessly the while), not merely because
part of my being had been violated and annulled,
but because all these many poems over the years
have been necessary—suitable and correct. This
has been the time of the finishing off of the animals.
They are going away—their fur and their wild eyes,
their voices. Deer leap and leap in front
of the screaming snowmobiles until they leap
out of existence. Hawks circle once or twice
above their shattered nests and then they climb
to the stars. I have lived with them fifty years,
we have lived with them fifty million years,
and now they are going, almost gone. I don't know
if the animals are capable of reproach.
But clearly they do not bother to say good-bye.

The Joy and Agony of Improvisation

There, the moon, just appearing
over dark pines, heavy and round,
the color of old parchment; and indeed
it seems archaic. What does it mean
in our histories, yours and mine,
except a myth no longer altogether
necessary, a theorem proven in another
millennium? This is a peculiar night,
uncomfortable. Well, it is like most moments
of the present, it doesn't fit us.
The low night wind, shifting, directionless,
moves the pine boughs, as if—so you say—
we were in the midst of voices in some
obscure contention. Of course we are.
But not obscure, only fruitless, stupid,
and very dangerous. Come,
let's go in the tent and sleep.

                    Later
we waken, knowing the night has changed.
It's a high wind now. Strange how the voices
have turned to song. Hear
it rising, rising, then breaking, then
rising again, and breaking again. Oh, something
is unutterable, the song cannot reach it.
Yet we know it, know what we cannot
hear—out on the night's great circle,

the circle of consciousness with its far rim always
hidden, there where suffering and joy
meet and combine,
the inexpressible. How the song is striving
and how beautifully failing—the measure
of beauty, beyond plenitude,
never but always enough. Come
outside again, under tossing pines
and the racing clouds. This
is more than we could ever have meant
in our kiss; it is the gathering of our love
into all love, into that suffering and joy.
And see, up there in the sky, uncovered now
as the clouds stream away,
the moon,
so new, so clean and high and bright and true.

Essay on Stone

April abomination, that's what I call
this wet snow sneaking down day after day,
    down the edges of air, when we
        were primed for spring.

The flowers of May will come next week—in theory.
And I suppose that witty sentimentalist,
    Heine, saw this same snow falling
        in the North Sea

as into the Abyss. I look out now across
this pasture, the mud and wet matted grass,
    the waving billows of it, where
        the snow is falling

as into our own abyss. I stand on Marshall's
great rock, to which I have returned, fascinated,
    a thousand times. I stand as if
        on a headland

or on an islet in the midst of waves,
and what is this fascination, this cold desire?
    Once I wrote a poem about
        making love to stone

and a whole book in which the protagonist,
who was myself, carried a stone with him
    everywhere he went. I still like
        that poem and that book,

and yet for all my years of stone-loving
I've learned not much about stone. Oh,
    I can tell slate from quartz from sandstone—
        who couldn't?—and here

in this district we even have an exotic
stone, the talc, that feels warm and bloody
    in one's hand, but basically I am
        ignorant. Let

the geologists keep their igneous pyrites
to themselves. I don't even know if
    this great rock, projecting
        bigger than a barn

from the slope of the pasture, is a free
boulder that may have come here from the top
    of Butternut Mountain who knows
        how many eons ago,

or part of the underlying granite of Vermont.
I stand on its back, looking into the abyss.
    At all events the fascination
        is undeniable. I

always said there could be no absolutes,
but this is stone, stone, stone—
    so here, so perfectly
        here. It is

the abyss inverted, the abyss made visible.
Years ago when I wrote that other poem
    I might have taken pleasure from this,
        I think I would have. Now

I am fifty-three going on fifty-four,
a rotten time of life. My end-of-winter clothes
    are threadbare, my boots cracked, and how
        astonishing to see

my back, like that figure in Rembrandt's drawing,
bent. I shift weight on my walking-stick
    and the stick slips in wet lichen
        and then my boots skid too,

and down I go—not hurt, just shaken.
And what a hurt that is! Is it consoling
    to know I might have fallen
        into the abyss?

All this in silence, every word of it spoken
in my mind. The snow falls. Heine,
    there must be something wrong with us.
        I've heard this pasture

moaning at my feet for years, as you heard
that gray sea, we two shaken and always
    unconsoled by what we love,
        the absolute stone.

John Dryden

Dry they call him, and dry is what he hopes
never to be, though springwater is all his drink
six nights after the welfare comes, and most
all his feed too, I sometimes think—though once
I saw him bring down a hare at seven rods
with a stone, and it didn't look lucky either.
When I asked him if he knew a famous poet
had the same name, he looked at me not quite
contemptuously; and yet I took a while to see
his scorn wasn't because he was smarter than I'd
credited—for a fact he can't read but about
half what's printed on the welfare check—but rather
because he's been asked so damn many times before
and he figured I should have known. I should have too.
Dry is not dumb. He's only crazy. Well, anyway
that's the general impression around the Plot,
which is what they call this section. My neighbor
rounds up her kids and locks her door when Dry
comes striding and caroling up the hill from town
in his outsize rummage pants with a carton
of grub held like an offering in both arms and his coat
gone slantywise from the fifth of sauterne
in his pocket. Paranoid, I'd say. There's more
than a few in these mountains, and sometimes I'm not
just certain about myself. But I know Dry.
I know he hasn't worked four consecutive days
on any one job in fifteen years. That's

indicative. Once we were haying up at Marshall's
and Dry took offense because a car with a shield
on the door drove in the barnyard and Dry thought
Marshall was telling the CIA on him, and he
came after Marshall and me with his hayfork,
chasing us round the tractor, his face dead white
like snow that's thawed and frozen again; he did,
and it wasn't funny either. My kidneys ached
two hours after from thinking about that fork.
Finally he saw he couldn't catch us. He threw down
the fork and marched off, straight as a bee, over
the meadow, the pasture, the orchard, the fence, and was gone.
That year Marshall and I made the rest of the hay
alone. One time Gilbert told how he and Dry
were cutting sugarwood for old man Saunders
up toward Codding Hollow, and Dry took one
of his spells and came after Gilbert with the axe,
and Gilbert yanked quick on his chainsaw string and remarked,
"Dry, you damn fool, listen here—just you set down
that thing, or by the jumping Jesus Christ
I'll cut off both your arms." Dry set it down,
about three inches into a black birch stump, and marched
straight as a bee over brakes and brambles,
hobblebush and thornapple, and he was gone.
Which may be indicative too; he can be "took"
right sudden, but when he's licked he knows it.
And he's a fair hand at marching. He told me once
how it was here forty years back. "Them days
was cruel," he said, "awful cruel. Things was
turning on a slow reel"—and he made a motion

like so, like the bobbins down to the woollen mill
when they run half-speed. "Why hell," he said,
"I had one of them five-dollar gold certificates,
you remember? I felt like I was rich, and I was too,
but I spent it running the cunt. And it come back,
and I spent it again, and it come back again,
so help me over and over till the damn thing
wore itself out—I carried the pieces for years.
But they're gone now." One time Dry vanished,
clean gone, no one knew where and don't know yet,
but when he came back I met him up in the woods
and he stood on a spruce log and threw out his arms
and said, "God, Hayden, it's Moxie in the can,
being back on this here goddamn mountain again!"
And he laughed. The last what you could call steady
job Dry had, as far as I know, was 1945
down at the rendering plant in Burlington where he
slugged cows with an axe and pushed their guts
through a hole in the floor all day. "Stink? Jesus,
I guess I stunk! Like a she bear in whistling time,
but I made good money. Forty a week, and that
wan't bad in them days; but I spent it all
running the cunt, every dime. Why, I got
throwed out of five flea-bag rooming houses
and I wan't even drunk, just owed the landlady
a week or two." Well, running's what we say
a bull does when you turn him out to pasture
with the cows, so you can see how Dry felt about that—
at least providing you've ever watched a bull
in action. "But now, goddamn it"—Dry spit

and grinned sly-like with his uppers, which is all
the teeth I've ever seen him wear—"now
you could lay a slobbering big juicy one right there,
right there ready and open"—him leaning and making
a kind of slicing gesture along the log—
"and I couldn't do nothing, I couldn't touch it,
couldn't hardly spit on it," and he spit and grinned.
"It'd be all wasted, Hayden. I'm fucked, fucked,
and I ain't but fifty-nine—how old are you?"
That's Dry all right. The nailhead every time.

Well, he lives up in the old Connell sugarhouse now
that he's shingled all over with sap bucket covers
to keep the wind out, till it looks like a big tin fish
in among the pines near the brook, and there's plenty
more he could tell you, like how he got bit that time
by the cattle grub and took the "purple aguey,"
or how he has a buckshot in him that keeps going
round and round in his veins, catching him sharp-like
on his cotterbone when he don't expect it
every now and again, or how he eats forty aspirins
a day and hears sweet patooty music in his ears,
or how he fell in a cellarhole at blackberrying time
and landed on a bear—"I says, 'Whuff, old bear,
get you away from me,' and then I climm the hell
out of there"—or how... but have you noticed
I can't talk *about* him without talking *like* him?
That's my trouble. Somehow I always seem
to turn into the other guy, and Dry's the kind
that brings it out the strongest. But *his* trouble

is what I'm telling about now; for it's not
just buckshot in his blood, it's worse, a whole
lot worse. His reel is turning slower and slower,
no mistake. Crazy? I reckon he is. I sure don't
want to be there when he's took bad, even now—
if he's got a fork or an axe within grabbing distance.
But I'll go up to call on him in his sugarhouse.
I believe old Dry is preparing to march again,
or anyway preparing to prepare. And I believe
he'll go straight as a bee, white as a squall of snow,
knowing what he damn well knows, over
the goldenrod, the birchwoods, the pines and hemlocks,
over the mountain. And he'll be gone. And then
Marshall and I shall make this hay alone,
by God, and curse old Dry. But in our thoughts
we'll remember and remember how that man could march.

Johnny Spain's White Heifer

The first time ever I saw Johnny Spain was
the first time I came to this town. There
he was, lantern jaw and broken nose, wall-eyed and
fractious, with a can of beer in one hand and a
walkie-talkie in the other, out in front
of the post office. And I heard someone saying,
"Johnny, what in hell are you doing?" "I'm looking,"
he answered, in an executive tone, "for me goddamn
white heifer." "Run off, did she?" "Yass,"
he said. "Busted me south-side fence, the bitch—
if some thieving bastard didn't bust it for her."
"You reckon she's running loose on Main Street?"
Johnny looked down, then up, then sideways, or possibly
all three together. "Hell, no," he growled.
"She's off there somewheres." He swung his beer can
in a circle. "Me boys is up in the hills, looking.
I'm di-recting the search." Then he turned away
to a crackle on the walkie-talkie.
                                        And that
was how Johnny liked it. He wasn't much
on farming, although his farm could have been
a fine one—closest to town, up on the hillside
overlooking the feed mill. But Johnny's curse
was a taste for administration. The "farm" was no more
than a falling-down barn, some mixed head
of cattle, and a flock of muddy ducks. Johnny
was the first man in the volunteer fire department
to have one of those revolving blue lights

set up on top of his car, and Johnny Spain
was *always* going to a fire. When he came down
off that hill of his in that air-borne '65 Pontiac—
look out! It was every man for himself
when Johnny was on the highway.
                                        I used to think
sometimes I had a glimpse of that white heifer
that Johnny never found. "A goddamn beauty,"
he'd say. "By Jesus, she was. Why, I give
five whole greenback dollars cash and a pair
of Indian runners to Blueball Baxter for her
when she were a calf—there wan't a finer heifer
in the whole goddamn county." I'd see a flash
of white in the balsams at the upper end of the pasture
or in the thickets across the brook when I looked up
at twilight; but I never found her. Probably
all I saw was a deer-tail flashing.
                                        After
they changed the town dump into a sanitary
landfill operation the selectmen hired Johnny
for custodian, and they gave him a little Michigan
dozer to bury the trash with. Johnny loved it.
"Dump it over there," he'd holler. "Goddamn it,
can't you see the sign? Tires and metal
go on the other side." One time he even
inaugurated a system of identification cards,
so people from Centerville and Irishtown
would quit using our dump, and by God
you had to show your pass, even if Johnny
had known you for years. Part of the deal

was salvage, of course. Johnny could take
whatever he wanted from the accumulated junk
and sell it. Trouble was he mostly didn't
or couldn't sell it, so it wound up in his
barnyard, everything from busted baby carriages
to stacks of old lard kegs from the diner,
up there to be viewed by whoever cared to look.
And the one with the best view was Mel Barstow,
son of the mill owner, who lived on the hill
above the other side of town. There they were,
two barons above the burg, facing each other
at opposite ends, like the West Wind and the East Wind
on an old-time map. Mel had everything
he thought he wanted—a home like a two-page spread
in *House and Garden*, for instance, and a wife
that was anyone's envy, and a pair of binoculars
with which he liked to watch the gulls flying
over the river. Of course he'd seen Johnny's place
many a time, but one evening he focused down
on that barnyard, then quick got on the phone.
"Johnny, why in hell don't you clean up that mess
over there? It's awful. It's a disgrace." Johnny
didn't say much. But a couple of nights later,
maybe about an hour past dark, he phoned up Mel.
"Mel," he said, "I got me a pair of them by-
nockyewlars over to Morrisville this forenoon,
and I been a-studying them goddamn birds out there,
and what I want to know is why in the hell
you don't tell that good-looking female of yours
to put some clothes on her backside when she's parading

up and down behind that picture window? Picture, hell—
I'll say it's a picture! It's a goddamn frigging
dis-grace, if you want to know the truth."

                                        Well,
I expect for a while Mel's wife was the one
that would have liked to get lost, and maybe
Mel too, because it's a cinch you can't go down
to buy even a pack of Winstons at the IGA
without running into Johnny Spain, and of course
Johnny's the one that knows exactly, exactly
how to keep the sting alive, winking wall-eyed
both ways at once, grinning that three-toothed grin.

But Johnny Spain's white heifer was what was lost.
She wasn't found. Wherever she is, she's gone.
Oh, I'm not the only one who thought they saw her,
because reports kept coming in, all the way round
from the Old Settlement clear up to Mariveau's
gravel pit. But that's all they were, just
reports. She'd have made a first-rate cow,
I reckon, if a man could have caught her, only
of course somewhat more than a mite wild.

Marshall Washer

I

They are cowshit farmers, these New Englanders
who built our red barns so admired as emblems,
in photograph, in paint, of America's imagined
past (backward utopians that we've become).
But let me tell how it is inside those barns.
Warm. Even in dead of winter, even in the
dark night solid with thirty below, thanks
to huge bodies breathing heat and grain sacks
stuffed under doors and in broken windows, warm,
and heaped with reeking, steaming manure, running
with urine that reeks even more, the wooden channels
and flagged aisles saturated with a century's
excreta. In dim light, with scraper and shovel,
the manure is lifted into a barrow or a trolley
(suspended from a ceiling track), and moved
to the spreader—half a ton at a time. Grain
and hay are distributed in the mangers, bedding
of sawdust strewn on the floor. The young cattle
and horses, separately stabled, are tended. The cows
are milked; the milk is strained and poured
in the bulk tank; the machines and all utensils
are washed with disinfectant. This, which is called
the "evening chores," takes about three hours.
Next morning, do it again. Then after breakfast
hitch the manure spreader to the old Ferguson

and draw it to the meadows, where the manure
is kicked by mechanical beaters onto the snow.
When the snow becomes too deep for the tractor,
often about mid-January, then load the manure
on a horse-drawn sled and pitch it out by hand.
When the snow becomes too deep for the horses
make your dung heap behind the barn. Yes, a good
winter means no dung heap; but a bad one
may mean a heap as big as a house. And so,
so, night and morning and day, 365 days
a year until you are dead; this is part
of what you must do. Notice how many times
I have said "manure"? It is serious business.
It breaks the farmers' backs. It makes their land.
It is the link eternal, binding man and beast
and earth. Yet our farmers still sometimes say
of themselves, derogatively, that they are "cowshit
farmers."

2

     I see a man with a low-bent back
driving a tractor in stinging rain, or just as he
enters a doorway in his sheepskin and enormous
mittens, stomping snow from his boots, raising
his fogged glasses. I see a man in bib overalls
and rubber boots kneeling in cowshit to smear
ointment on a sore teat, a man with a hayfork,
a dungfork, an axe, a 20-pound maul

for driving posts, a canthook, a grease gun.
I see a man notching a cedar post
with a double-blade axe, rolling the post
under his foot in the grass: quick strokes and there
is a ringed groove one inch across, as clean
as if cut with the router blade down at the mill.
I see a man who drags a dead calf or watches
a barn roaring with fire and thirteen heifers
inside, I see his helpless eyes. He has stood
helpless often, of course: when his wife died
from congenital heart disease a few months before
open-heart surgery came to Vermont, when his sons
departed, caring little for the farm because
he had educated them—he who left school
in 1931 to work by his father's side
on an impoverished farm in an impoverished time.
I see a man who studied by lamplight, the journals
and bulletins, new methods, struggling to buy
equipment, forty years to make his farm
a good one; alone now, his farm the last
on Clay Hill, where I myself remember ten.
He says "I didn't mind it" for "I didn't notice it,"
"dreened" for "drained," "climb" (pronounced *climm*)
for "climbed," "stanchel" for "stanchion,"
and many other unfamiliar locutions; but I
have looked them up, they are in the dictionary,
standard speech of lost times. He is rooted
in history as in the land, the only man I know
who lives in the house where he was born. I see
a man alone walking his fields and woods,

knowing every useful thing about them, moving
in a texture of memory that sustains his lifetime
and his father's lifetime. I see a man
falling asleep at night with thoughts and dreams
I could not infer—and would not if I could—
in his chair in front of the television.

3

                                        I have written
of Marshall often, for his presence is in my poems
as in my life, so familiar that it is not named;
yet I have named him sometimes too, in writing
as in life, gratefully. We are friends. Our friendship
began when I came here years ago, seeking
what I had once known in southern New England,
now destroyed. I found it in Marshall, among others.
He is friend and neighbor both, an important
distinction. His farm is one-hundred-eighty acres
(plus a separate woodlot of forty more), and one
of the best-looking farms I know, sloping smooth
pastures, elm-shaded knolls, a brook, a pond,
his woods of spruce and pine, with maples and oaks
along the road—not a showplace, not by any means,
but a working farm with fences of old barbed wire;
no pickets, no post-and-rail. His cows are Jerseys.
My place, no farm at all, is a country laborer's
holding, fourteen acres "more or less" (as the deed
says), but we adjoin. We have no fence. Marshall's

cows graze in my pasture; I cut my fuel
in his woods. That's neighborliness. And when
I came here Marshall taught me... I don't know,
it seems like everything: how to run a barn,
make hay, build a wall, make maple syrup
without a trace of bitterness, a thousand things.
(Though I thought I wasn't ignorant when I came,
and I wasn't—just three-quarters informed.
You know how good a calf is, born three-legged.)
In fact half my life now, I mean literally half,
is spent in actions I could not perform without
his teaching. Yet it wasn't teaching; he *showed* me.
Which is what makes all the difference. In return
I gave a hand, helped in the fields, started
frozen engines, mended fence, searched for lost calves,
picked apples for the cider mill, and so on.
And Marshall, now alone, often shared my table.
This too is neighborliness.

4

As for friendship,
what can I say where words historically fail?
It is something else, something more difficult. Not
western affability, at any rate, that tells
in ten minutes the accommodation of its wife's—well,
you know. Yankees are independent, meaning
individual and strong-minded but also private;
in fact private first of all. Marshall and I

worked ten years together, and more than once
in hardship. I remember the late January
when his main gave out and we carried water,
hundreds and thousands of gallons, to the heifers
in the upper barn (the one that burned next summer),
then worked inside the well to clear the line
in temperatures that rose to ten below
at noonday. We knew such times. Yet never
did Marshall say the thought that was closest to him.
Privacy is what this is; not reticence, not
minding one's own business, but a positive sense
of the secret inner man, the sacred identity.
A man is his totem, the animal of his mind.
Yet I was angered sometimes. How could friendship
share a base so small of mutual substance?
Unconsciously I had taken friendship's measure
from artists elsewhere who had been close to me,
people living for the minutest public dissection
of emotion and belief. But more warmth was,
and is, in Marshall's quiet "hello" than in all
those others and their wordiest protestations,
more warmth and far less vanity.

    5

                    He sows
his millet broadcast, swinging left to right,
a half-acre for the cows' "fall tonic" before
they go in the barn for good; an easy motion,

slow swinging, a slow dance in the field, and just
the opposite, right to left, for the scythe
or the brush-hook. Yes, I have seen such dancing
by a man alone in the slant of the afternoon.
At his anvil with his big smith's hammer
he can pound shape back in a wagon iron, or tap
a butternut so it just lies open. When he skids
a pine log out of the woods he stands in front
of his horse and hollers, "Gee-up, goddamn it,"
"Back, you ornery son-of-a-bitch," and then
when the chain rattles loose and the log settles
on the stage, he slicks down the horse's sweaty
neck and pulls his ears. In October he eases
the potatoes out of the ground in their rows,
gentle with the potato-hook, then leans and takes
a big one in his hand, and rubs it clean
with his thumbs, and smells it, and looks
along the new-turned frosty earth to fields,
to hills, to the mountain, forests in their color
each fall no less awesome. And when in June
the mowing time comes around and he fits the wicked
cutter-bar to the Ferguson, he shuts the cats
indoors, the dogs in the barn, and warns
the neighbors too, because once years ago,
many years, he cut off a cat's legs in the tall
timothy. To this day you can see him
squirm inside when he tells it, as he must tell it,
obsessively, June after June. He is tall,
a little gray, a little stooped, his eyes
crinkled with smile-lines, both dog-teeth gone.

He has worn his gold-rimmed spectacles so long
he looks disfigured when they're broken.

6

                                        No doubt
Marshall's sorrow is the same as human
sorrow generally, but there is this
difference. To live in a doomed city, a doomed
nation, a doomed world is desolating, and we all,
all are desolated. But to live on a doomed farm
is worse. It must be worse. There the exact
point of connection, gate of conversion, is—
mind and life. The hilltop farms are going.
Bottomland farms, mechanized, are all that survive.
As more and more developers take over
northern Vermont, values of land increase,
taxes increase, farming is an obsolete vocation—
while half the world goes hungry. Marshall walks
his fields and woods, knowing every useful thing
about them, and knowing his knowledge useless.
Bulldozers, at least of the imagination,
are poised to level every knoll, to strip bare
every pasture. Or maybe a rich man will buy it
for a summer place. Either way the link
of the manure, that had seemed eternal, is broken.
Marshall is not young now. And though I am only
six or seven years his junior, I wish somehow
I could buy the place, merely to assure him

that for these few added years it might continue—
drought, flood, or depression. But I am too
ignorant, in spite of his teaching. This is more
than a technocratic question. I cannot smile
his quick sly Yankee smile in sorrow,
nor harden my eyes with the true granitic resistance
that shaped this land. How can I learn the things
that are not transmissible? Marshall knows them.
He possesses them, the remnant of human worth
to admire in this world, and I think to envy.

The Poet

All night his window
shines in the woods
shadowed under the hills
where the gray owl

is hunting. He hears
the woodmouse scream—
so small a sound
in the great darkness

entering his pain.
For he is all and all
of pain, attracting
every new injury

to be taken and borne
as he must take
and bear it. He is
nothing; he is

his admiration. So
they seem almost
to know—the woodmouse
and the roving owl,

the woods and hills.
All night they move
around the stillness
of the poet's light.

FROM *If You Call This Cry a Song* (1983)

On Being Asked to Write a Poem
Against the War in Vietnam

Well I have and in fact
more than one and I'll
tell you this too

I wrote one against
Algeria that nightmare
and another against

Korea and another
against the one
I was in

and I don't remember
how many against
the three

when I was a boy
Abyssinia Spain and
Harlan County

and not one
breath was restored
to one

shattered throat
mans womans or childs
not one not

one
but death went on and on
never looking aside

except now and then like a child
with a furtive half-smile
to make sure I was noticing.

Regarding Chainsaws

The first chainsaw I owned was years ago,
an old yellow McCulloch that wouldn't start.
Bo Bremmer give it to me that was my friend,
though I've had enemies couldn't of done
no worse. I took it to Ward's over to Morrisville,
and no doubt they tinkered it as best they could,
but it still wouldn't start. One time later
I took it down to the last bolt and gasket
and put it together again, hoping somehow
I'd do something accidental-like that would
make it go, and then I yanked on it
450 times, as I figured afterwards,
and give myself a bursitis in the elbow
that went five years even after
Doc Arrowsmith shot it full of cortisone
and near killed me when he hit a nerve
dead on. Old Stan wanted that saw, wanted it bad.
Figured I was a greenhorn that didn't know
nothing and he could fix it. Well, I was,
you could say, being only forty at the time,
but a fair hand at tinkering. "Stan," I said,
"you're a neighbor. I like you. I wouldn't
sell that thing to nobody, except maybe
Vice-President Nixon." But Stan persisted.
He always did. One time we was loafing and
gabbing in his front dooryard, and he spied
that saw in the back of my pickup. He run

quick inside, then come out and stuck a double
sawbuck in my shirt pocket, and he grabbed
that saw and lugged it off. Next day, when I
drove past, I seen he had it snugged down tight
with a tow-chain on the bed of his old Dodge
Powerwagon, and he was yanking on it
with both hands. Two or three days after,
I asked him, "How you getting along with that
McCulloch, Stan?" "Well," he says, "I tooken
it down to scrap, and I buried it in three
separate places yonder on the upper side
of the potato piece. You can't be too careful,"
he says, "when you're disposing of a hex."
The next saw I had was a godawful ancient
Homelite that I give Dry Dryden thirty bucks for,
temperamental as a ram too, but I liked it.
It used to remind me of Dry and how he'd
clap that saw a couple times with the flat
of his double-blade axe to make it go
and how he honed the chain with a worn-down
file stuck in an old baseball. I worked
that saw for years. I put up forty-five
run them days each summer and fall to keep
my stoves het through the winter. I couldn't now.
It'd kill me. Of course they got these here
modern Swedish saws now that can take
all the worry out of it. What's the good
of that? Takes all the fun out too, don't it?
Why, I reckon. I mind when Gilles Boivin snagged

an old sap spout buried in a chunk of maple
and it tore up his mouth so bad he couldn't play
"Tea for Two" on his cornet in the town band
no more, and then when Toby Fox was holding
a beech limb that Rob Bowen was bucking up
and the saw skidded crossways and nipped off
one of Toby's fingers. Ain't that more like it?
Makes you know you're living. But mostly they wan't
dangerous, and the only thing they broke was your
back. Old Stan, he was a buller and a jammer
in his time, no two ways about that, but he
never sawed himself. Stan had the sugar
all his life, and he wan't always too careful
about his diet and the injections. He lost
all the feeling in his legs from the knees down.
One time he started up his Powerwagon
out in the barn, and his foot slipped off the clutch,
and she jumped forwards right through the wall
and into the manure pit. He just set there,
swearing like you could of heard it in St.
Johnsbury, till his wife come out and said,
"Stan, what's got into you?" "Missus," he says
"ain't nothing got into me. Can't you see?
It's me that's got into this here pile of shit."
Not much later they took away one of his
legs, and six months after that they took
the other and left him setting in his old chair
with a tank of oxygen to sip at whenever
he felt himself sinking. I remember that chair.

Stan reupholstered it with an old bearskin
that must of come down from his great-great-
grandfather and had grit in it left over
from the Civil War and a bullet-hole as big
as a yawning cat. Stan latched the pieces together
with rawhide, cross fashion, but the stitches was
always breaking and coming undone. About then
I quit stopping by to see old Stan, and I
don't feel so good about that neither. But my mother
was having her strokes then. I figured
one person coming apart was as much
as a man can stand. Then Stan was taken away
to the nursing home, and then he died. I always
remember how he planted them pieces of spooked
McCulloch up above the potatoes. One time
I went up and dug, and I took the old
sprocket, all pitted and et away, and set it
on the windowsill right there next to the
butter mold. But I'm damned if I know why.

Song of the Two Crows

I sing of Morrisville
(if you call this cry
    a song). I
(if you call this painful

voice by that great name)
sing the poverty of my
    region and of
the wrong end of Morrisville.

You summer people will say
that all its ends are wrong,
    but there, right there,
the very end of the wrong end—

a house with windows sagging,
leaning roadward as in defense
    or maybe defiance
next to the granite ledge,

our cliff of broken stone
that shoulders our dilapidated
    one-lane iron bridge.
Who lives here? I don't know.

But they (Hermes reward them)
made this extraordinary garden,
    geraniums,
petunias and nasturtiums

planted in every crevice and all
the footholds of the cliff.
    And then
they painted the cliff-face,

painted the old stone; no design,
just swatches of color, bold
    rough splashes
irregularly, garish orange

and livid blue. Is it
fluorescent, do these stones
    glow in the dark?
Maybe. I only know

they glow in the day, so
vivid I stopped my car,
    whereupon two others
came inquiring also, two

crows in the broken spars
of the white pine tree, cawing
    above the house.
Why had those who inhabited

this corner of poverty
painted the stones? Was it
    that the flowers
in living bravery nevertheless

made too meager a show
for the ruined cliff? Or did they
    think to bring art
to nature, somehow to improve

this corner of ugliness?
For my part I thought how
    these colors
were beautiful and yet strange

in their beauty, ugly colors,
garish orange, livid blue;
    they reminded me
of those Spanish cemeteries

I saw in New Mexico, tin
mirrors and plastic flowers
    in the desert. Then
I knew why the stones

had been painted: to make
reparation, such as the poor
    might make, whose sorrow
had been done here, this

.

desecration. Is not this
the burden of all poor lands
    everywhere,
the basis of poverty?

A spoiled land makes spoiled
people. The poor know this.
    I guess
the crows know too, because off

they flew, cawing above
the bridge and the slashed hills
    surrounding Morrisville.
I started my car and drove

out on the iron bridge
which rumbled its sullen
    affirmation.
And I sang as I sing now

(if you care to call it song)
my people of Morrisville
    who live
where all the ends are wrong.

The Oldest Killed Lake in North America

One night the water lay so deathly still
that the factories' constellated lights on the other shore,
the mills and refineries, made gleaming wires
across the surface, a great fallen and silent
harp; and the moon, huge and orange,
shuddered behind the trembling many-petaled efflorescence
on the stalks of the chimneys, white mortuary flowers.
Really, from the nearer shore on the highway to Liverpool,
one saw the kind of splendor that lasts forever.

Sometimes When Lovers Lie Quietly Together, Unexpectedly One of Them Will Feel the Other's Pulse

'Tis just beyond mid-August. The summer has run mockingly
    away, as usual.
The first equinoctial storm has killed a certain paltry number
    of innocents in Galveston, who will be hardly missed,
And now its remnant brings a wind to Syracuse, a zephyrous
    wind that clears the air a little.
Not much. Haze lingers over the Bradford Hills.
What the Preacher said about retribution is true, true in the
    very nature of things, and therefore we Middle Americans
    must pay now
For our sins. Standing by the kitchen window, I escaped into
    my woodland soul
Where I saw our willow, the great eastern Maenad, *Salix
babylonica*, toss her wild hair in sexual frenzy.
Then I went to my chair in the living room. I drank coffee and
    smoked, the relentless daily struggle to awaken.
Above the street at heavy opalescent noontime two electrical
    cables, strung from pole to pole,
Hung in relationship to one another such that the lower swung
    in and out of the shadow of the one above it,
And as it did so the sunlight reflected from it was sprung
    gleaming outward and inward along its length,
A steady expansion and contraction. And for a while I was
    taken away from my discontents
By this rhythm of the truth of the world, so fundamental, so
    simple, so clear.

The Impossible Indispensability of the *Ars Poetica*

But of course the poem is not an assertion. Do you see? When
    I wrote
That all my poems over the long years before I met you made
    you come true,
And that the poems for you since then have made you in
    yourself become more true,
I did not mean that the poems created or invented you. How
    many have foundered
In that sargasso! No, what I have been trying to say
For all the years of my awakening
Is that neither of the quaint immemorial views of poetry is
    adequate for us.
A poem is not an expression, nor is it an object. Yet it
    somewhat partakes of both. What a poem is
Is never to be known, for which I have learned to be grateful.
    But the aspect in which I see my own
Is as the act of love. The poem is a gift, a bestowal.
The poem is for us what instinct is for animals, a continuing
    and chiefly unthought corroboration of essence
(Though thought, ours and the animals', is still useful).
Why otherwise is the earliest always the most important, the
    formative? The *Iliad*, the *Odyssey*, the book of Genesis,
These were acts of love, I mean deeply felt gestures, which
    continuously bestow upon us
What we are. And if I do not know which poem of mine
Was my earliest gift to you,
Except that it had to have been written about someone else,

Nevertheless it was the gesture accruing value to you, your
        essence, while you were still a child, and thereafter
Across all these years. And see, see how much
Has come from that first sonnet after our loving began, the
        one
That was a kiss, a gift, a bestowal. This is the paradigm of
        fecundity. I think the poem is not
Transparent, as some have said, nor a looking-glass, as some
        have also said,
Yet it has almost the quality of disappearance
In its cage of visibility. It disperses among the words. It is a
        fluidity, a vapor, of love.
This, the instinctual, is what caused me to write "Do you see?"
        instead of "Don't you see?" in the first line
Of this poem, this loving treatise, which is what gives away the
        poem
And gives it all to you.

Of Distress Being Humiliated by the Classical Chinese Poets

Masters, the mock orange is blooming in Syracuse without
     scent, having been bred by patient horticulturalists
To make this greater display at the expense of fragrance.
But I miss the jasmine of my back-country home.
Your language has no tenses, which is why your poems can
     never be translated whole into English;
Your minds are the minds of men who feel and imagine
     without time.
The serenity of the present, the repose of my eyes in the cool
     whiteness of sterile flowers.
Even now the headsman with his great curved blade and rank
     odor is stalking the byways for some of you.
When everything happens at once, no conflicts can occur.
Reality is an impasse. Tell me again
How the white heron rises from among the reeds and flies
     forever across the nacreous river at twilight
Toward the distant islands.

Survival as Tao, Beginning at 5:00 A.M.

Shadows in the room. Strange objects. The gladiolas on the
    coffee table, for instance,
The pink, deep red, yellow, and tangerine, these are all now
    more or less tropical and black,
Somehow menacing in the huge earthenware pitcher, which
    resembles a sea anemone.
Three small mantas swim through. Insomnia, the *demonstratus*
    of the ground of despair,
Mixed with several kinds of tranquilizers: the mantas are not
    unexpected,
Nor is this atavistic sense of elsewhere. What is unexpected
Is this sentence by Leibnitz: "Music is an exercise in
    metaphysics while the mind does not know it is
    philosophizing."
I ought to look up the original, I do not care for
The word *exercise*, I suspect an infelicitous translation.
L. himself was seldom infelicitous. But never mind the words
    for once, the statement catches at something
True and important. Music is the attempt to survive the
    unbearable through freedom from objectivity
Bestowed from outside, i.e., by the variable frequencies of
    sound waves.
Loving, on the other hand, is an exercise, so-called, in
    metaphysics while the mind is perfectly aware,
For sex would be merely an objective conduct, an addiction,
    without the intellect to discover the meanings
Implicitly always in it. Loving is to survive the unbearable
    through freedom bestowed

From the inside, mutually. It is the only functional exercise in
        metaphysics still enduring, still
Enjoining our otherwise denatured sensibilities to perceive and
        understand the positive aspects of Being,
As the dawnlight indicates. The mantas swim away. The
        gladiolas, smiling lugubriously,
Deposit the unbearable upon the day, that is, their lower
        blossoms, withered overnight.
Coffee and cigarettes in my Chinese bathrobe. The day,
        Sunday, will be hotter than yesterday, Saturday, which was
Hotter than the day before, Friday, etc. Now the child's
        television emits the most incredible
Noises I have ever heard. Where's the music? (*"Wo ist die
        Musik?"* the Bo said, so many years ago.) No one
Remembers how it was made, except I—*ego, scriptor.*
Yet in the freedom of orgasm my thought of the woman
Is indeed a song, a metaphysical song, soaring in the
        inconceivable, brought to the fullness of harmony
By her thought of me.

"Sure," said Benny Goodman,

"We rode out the depression on technique." How gratifying,
     how rare,
Such expressions of a proper modesty. Notice it was not said
By T. Dorsey, who could not play a respectable "Honeysuckle
     Rose" on a kazoo,
But by the man who turned the first jazz concert in Carnegie
     Hall
Into an artistic event and put black musicians on the stand with
     white ones equally,
The man who called himself Barefoot Jackson, or some such,
In order to be a sideman with Mel Powell on a small label
And made good music on "Blue Skies," etc. He knew exactly
     who he was, no more, no less.
It was rare and gratifying, as I've said. Do you remember the
     Incan priestling, Xtlgg, who said,
"O Lord Sun, we are probably not good enough to exalt thee,"
     and got himself
Flung over the wall at Machu Picchu for his candor?
I honor him for that, but I like him because his statement
     implies
That if he had foreseen the outcome he might not have said it.
But he did say it. *Candor seeks its own unforeseeable occasions.*
Once in America in a dark time the existentialist flatfoot floogie
     stomped across the land
Accompanied by a small floy floy. I think we shall not see their
     like in our people's art again.

FROM *Collected Shorter Poems,*
1946–1991 (1992)
New Poems (1986–1991)

Pa McCabe

You tell these young spratasses around here
you got a ram down in the brook, they'll look
at you like you was talking the Mongolian
jabberfizzy, they ain't never heard of any such
a thing. Even if you say it's a *hydraulic*
ram, it don't mean nothing to them. Maybe
it don't to you. Well, a ram is a kind of a pump,
see? It works without any power except the force
of the water itself. How? You're thinking I'm
off my rocker? Ok. You got an inlet pipe
that's four to five times the diameter of the
outlet, and you set that inlet far enough up
the brook so it makes a fall of maybe two to
three feet, so the incoming water will hit
with force. What happens is it hits a little
weighted valve and pushes it upwards so most
of the water sprays out and goes back to the brook.
But then the valve falls closed again from its
own weight, and that pushes a little water up
into the dome, and of course that creates pressure
same as you got in any pump, and the pressure
will drive some of the water into the outlet.
Ingenious, ain't it? Of course it ain't what you
guys would call efficient; you only get out
about 10 to 15 percent of the incoming water. But
it don't cost nothing! Nothing! No electricity,

no gasoline. Once you got that pump going, it'll run forever.

I had a small one once, borrowed off Marshall, and I set it up in the brook on a rock so it would pump a stream of water about the size of a pencil up to the garden. It worked fine. All night long I could hear that little valve going tap, tap, tap down there in the brook, working away for nothing but the pure joy of working, and that's something, if you take my meaning. Still a pencil of water don't spread itself around much, so I figured I needed a reservoir to catch it. Then I could fill my bucket from the reservoir instead of climbing down to the brook and back again, and spread that water even, where I needed it. I went up the road to see Pa McCabe. "You got any kind of drum," I said, "maybe forty gallon or so." Pa looked sidewise and pulled his ear. "Why," he says, "I got a old paint barrel holds 60 gallon. Trouble is it's still coated with paint on the inside." "I can burn it off with my torch," I said. "Yes, you could do that," he says. "What do you want for it?" I says. He turned his gaze up toward the mountaintop. "Why," he says, "how about three dollars?" I damn near exploded. Three dollars? I wouldn't have give three whole dollars for a copper dog that laid brass turds. But I seen that wan't the right approach, so to speak. "Done," I says. And I handed him three frogskins.

So I had that barrel in the back
of my pickup just outside the barn door, and I
begin to put her in gear, when Pa hollers at me,
"Hold on a minute, hold on," and he runs in the
house—the kind of running you do when you're
seventy-nine and three-and-a-half feet wide—
and in a couple of owlblinks he comes out
waving a half-gallon of syrup, worth a good
six-fifty at the going rate in them years.
"Here," he says, "take this home to your wife
and tell her it's from her hot old honey up in
the hill section." It were the onliest time I ever
seen old Pa so downright ashamed of himself.
I'm using that barrel yet. But of course
we drunk up the syrup. Syrup don't last long.

Pray You Young Woman

Pray you young woman come to my bed clean
And that your lover's dregs be drained away.
Come not quickly but leave time in between.
I'm old and waitful, I can stand delay
Better than that too clearly you'd betray
My doting. True. Sweetheart, you must be mean
A little, devious and deceitful, and not say
You come from him—I'll know. Just go, obscene
As ever you wish, play the long bright day
With his young body; then come, draw night's screen
Over me, pleasure me, let my decay
Be hidden. For your hands can touch gangrene
And make it seem like my green springtime still
In perjury and mercy if you will.

Assignment

"Then write," she said. "By all means, if that's
      how you feel about it. Write poems.
Write about the recurved arcs of my breasts
      joined in an angle at my nipples, how
the upper curve tilts toward the sky and the lower
      reverses sharply back into my torso,
write about how my throat rises from the supple
      hinge of my collarbones proudly so to speak
with the coin-sized hollow at the center, write
      of the perfect arch of my jaw when I hold
my head back—these are the things in which I too
      take delight—write how my skin is
fine like a cover of snow but warm and soft and
      fitted to me perfectly, write the *volupté*
of soap frothing in my curling crotch-hair, write
      the tight parabola of my vulva that re-
sembles a braided loop swung from a point,
      write the two dapples of light on the backs
of my knees, write my ankles so neatly turning
      in their sockets to deploy all the sweet
bones of my feet, write how when I am aroused
      I sway like a cobra and make sounds
of sucking with my mouth and brush my nipples
      with the tips of my left-hand fingers, and then
write how all this is continually pre-existing in my
      thought and how I effect it in myself

by my will, which you are not permitted to under-
stand. Do this. Do it in pleasure and with
devotion, and don't worry about time. I won't
need what you've done until you finish."

FROM *Scrambled Eggs & Whiskey:*
Poems, 1991–1995 (1996)

Birthday Cake

For breakfast I have eaten the last of your birthday cake that you
had left uneaten for five days
and would have left five more before throwing it away.
It is early March now. The winter of illness
is ending. Across the valley
patches of remaining snow make patterns among the hill farms,
among fields and knolls and woodlots,
like forms in a painting, as sure and significant as forms
in a painting. The cake was stale.
But I like stale cake, I even prefer it, which you don't
understand, as I don't understand how you can open
a new box of cereal when the old one is still unfinished.
So many differences. You a woman, I a man,
you still young at forty-two and I growing old at seventy.
Yet how much we love one another.
It seems a miracle. Not mystical, nothing occult,
just the ordinary improbability that occurs
over and over, the stupendousness
of life. Out on the highway on the pavement wet
with snow-melt, cars go whistling past.
And our poetry, yours short-lined and sounding
beautifully vulgar and bluesy
in your woman's bitterness, and mine almost
anything, unpredictable, though people say
too ready a harkening back
to the useless expressiveness and ardor of another
era. But how lovely it was, that time

in my restless memory.
This is the season of mud and trash, broken limbs and crushed briers
from the winter storms, wetness and rust,
the season of differences, articulable differences that signify
deeper and inarticulable and almost paleolithic
perplexities in our lives, and still
we love one another. We love this house
and this hillside by the highway in upstate New York.
I am too old to write love songs now. I no longer
assert that I love you, but that you love me,
confident in my amazement. The spring
will come soon. We will have more birthdays
with cakes and wine. This valley
will be full of flowers and birds.

Testament

So often has it been displayed to us, the hourglass
with its grains of sand drifting down,
not as an object in our world
but as a sign, a symbol, our lives
drifting down grain by grain,
sifting away—I'm sure everyone must
see this emblem somewhere in the mind.
Yet not only our lives drift down. The stuff
of ego with which we began, the mass
in the upper chamber, filters away
as love accumulates below. Now
I am almost entirely love. I have been
to the banker, the broker, those strange
people, to talk about unit trusts,
annuities, CDs, IRAs, trying
to leave you whatever I can after
I die. I've made my will, written
you a long letter of instructions.
I think about this continually.
What will you do? How
will you live? You can't go back
to cocktail waitressing in the casino.
And your poetry? It will bring you
at best a pittance in our civilization,
a widow's mite, as mine has
for forty-five years. Which is why
I leave you so little. Brokers?

Unit trusts? I'm no financier doing
the world's great business. And the sands
in the upper glass grow few. Can I leave
you the vale of ten thousand trilliums
where we buried our good cat Pokey
across the lane to the quarry?
Maybe the tulips I planted under
the lilac tree? Or our red-bellied
woodpeckers who have given us so
much pleasure, and the rabbits
and the deer? And kisses? And
love-makings? All our embracings?
I know millions of these will be still
unspent when the last grain of sand
falls with its whisper, its inconsequence,
on the mountain of my love below.

Ecstasy

For years it was in sex and I thought
this was the most of it
                    so brief

                            a moment
or two of transport out of oneself
                          or
in music which lasted longer and filled me
with the exquisite wrenching agony
of the blues
                and now it is equally
transitory and obscure as I sit in my broken
chair that the cats have shredded
by the stove on a winter night with wind and snow
howling outside and I imagine
the whole world at peace
                    at peace
and everyone comfortable and warm
the great pain assuaged
                            a moment
of the most shining and singular sensual gratification.

Prepare

"Why don't you write me a poem that will prepare me for your
   death?" you said.
It was a rare day here in our climate, bright and sunny. I didn't
   feel like dying that day,
I didn't even want to think about it—my lovely knees and bold
   shoulders broken open,
Crawling with maggots. Good Christ! I stood at the window
   and I saw a strange dog
Running in the field with its nose down, sniffing the snow,
   zigging and zagging,
And whose dog is that? I asked myself. As if I didn't know. The
   limbs of the apple trees
Were lined with snow, making a bright calligraphy against the
   world, messages to me
From an enigmatic source in an obscure language. Tell me,
   how shall I decipher them?
And a jay slanted down to the feeder and looked at me behind
   my glass and squawked.
Prepare, prepare. Fuck you, I said, come back tomorrow. And
   here he is in this new gray and gloomy morning.
We're back to our normal weather. Death in the air, the idea of
   death settling around us like mist,
And I am thinking again in despair, in desperation, how will it
   happen? Will you wake up
Some morning and find me lying stiff and cold beside you in
   our bed? How atrocious!
Or will I fall asleep in the car, as I nearly did a couple of weeks
   ago, and drive off the road

Into a tree? The possibilities are endless and not at all
    fascinating, except that I can't stop
Thinking about them, can't stop envisioning that moment of
    hideous violence.
Hideous and indescribable as well, because it won't happen
    until it's over. But not for you.
For you it will go on and on, thirty years or more, since that's
    the distance between us
In our ages. The loss will be a great chasm with no bridge
    across it (for we both know
Our life together, so unexpected, is entirely loving and rare).
    Living on your own—
Where will you go? What will you do? And the continuing
    sense of displacement
From what we've had in this little house, our refuge on our
    green or snowbound
Hill. *Life is not easy and you will be alive.* Experience reduces
    itself to platitudes always,
Including the one which says that I'll be with you forever in
    your memories and dreams.
I will. And also in hundreds of keepsakes, such as this scrap of
    a poem you are reading now.

FROM *Doctor Jazz* (2001)

Because I Am

in mem. Sidney Bechet, 1897–1959

Because I am a memorious old man
I've been asked to write about you, Papa Sidney,
Improvising in standard meter on a well-known
Motif, as you did all those nights in Paris
And the world. I remember once in Chicago
On the Near North where you were playing with
A white band, how you became disgusted
And got up and sat in front next to the bandstand
And ordered four ponies of brandy; and then
You drank them one by one, and threw the empty
Glasses at the trumpet-player. Everyone laughed,
Of course, but you were dead serious—sitting there
With your fuzzy white head, in your rumpled navy
Serge. When you lifted that brass soprano to your
Lips and blew, you were superb, the best of all,
The first and best, an *Iliad* to my ears.
And always your proper creole name was mis-
Pronounced. Now you are lost in the bad shadows
Of time past; you are a dark man in the darkness,
Who knew us all in music. Out of the future
I hear ten thousand saxophones mumbling
In your riffs and textures, Papa Sidney. And when
I stand up trembling in darkness to recite
I see sparkling glass ponies come sailing at me
Out of the reaches of the impermeable night.

The Sound

When I was a boy at this time of year
I lay on the near side of our small meadow
in the tall grass and listened to the bees
on the far side in the honey locust
trees. I couldn't see them, or the trees
either, hidden as I was in the grass,
but the sound was loud and somehow
sweet—the humming of innumerable
bees, as Tennyson would have said.
The sound seemed everywhere as I
gazed at the sky, enclosed in my sweet
grave in the grass. *This is how the sound
of the invisible stars singing would be,*
I said, *if only I could hear them.*

Dearest M—

The First Day of Her Death
(As Recorded by Her Father)

In November when the days are short and dim
     she died. In November
when the Baldwin apple tree retains
hundreds of its bright apples, each bejeweled
     with a sparkle of snow
     under our gray Oneidan sky,
she died. She was Martha. She was my daughter.

A strange, unnatural thing is it—to outlive
     one's daughter.
I go repeatedly, repeatedly, to stand and gaze
     out my window
as if with my glaring eye I could blast
the ornamented Baldwin into nonexistence
     and bring down all,
as if the tree were good and evil, as if
     the world meant something.
Yes, the waves and buffets of all humanity's
desperation shake me like a leaf,
     although I stand stock-still.

The immensity of what should be said
     defeats me. Language
like a dismasted hulk at sea is overwhelmed
     and founders.

Only last week Sappho
lay in the arms of some sleek adolescent
on her green and golden isle
and coughed—barked like a seal—
        and died.

And then a lifetime ago the pediatrician
examined her, eyes, ears, mouth,
heart and lungs, hands and feet, and finally
with expert thumbs he parted her tiny vulva
three days old, looked and stood back.
        "Perfect," he said. "She's perfect." Was this
the first of all of her triumphant indignities?

        In a cold puff of air, as if
thousands of invisible and soundless feet
        were marching by,
the apple tree sways briefly and stands still.

Looking "nearly weightless" (I was told) she lay
like a young crone,
        who had been as beautiful and sexy
as any young woman you could care to meet;
riddled with cancer, wracked by pneumonia,
comatose in a stupor of morphine, attached
by tubes and wires to the gleaming apparatus.
        And slowly
the intelligence receded from her eyes.

        Slowly the shadow fades
        from a footprint in the snow.

"Don't hurt the snow, don't hurt the snow!" she cried
as I pulled on my gloves and lifted
the shovel to my shoulder by the door,
she who became a painter and who now is
        the painter forever,
all these images of earthly splendor and fascination
        on our walls,
from here to California.

Three deer have come to the apple tree, pawing the snow
for fallen, frozen apples. One of them, a young doe,
rises on her bent back legs with her forelegs
hanging and helpless, to reach an apple on the tree,
        but she cannot—
this defeated, humble, supplicative gesture.
Yet even pathos remains futile. Can anything arouse
passion in an old man like the death of a young
woman? The desire to smash something,
        but what's the good
of littering the floor with splintered glass?
Nothing is worth smashing. And then,
out of character, beyond reason, it is
        sexual too.
The evil desire to fuck someone so that she'll
stay fucked once and for all. It's true, one thinks,
        God must be a female.
Who else would so humiliate a hungry doe?

Martha did her painting in private. We rarely
        saw her at work.

If by chance we did, she would stand pointedly
in front of her easel, shielding the canvas
from our view. Similarly, she did not talk
about her painting, perhaps because she was
self-taught and didn't know the words—
        but that's nonsense.
She was as language-driven as her father,
she had plenty of words. But process was
something she did not wish to discuss.
        Her paintings
were neither representational nor abstract.
She painted what she saw, supplying color and contrast
from the deepest recesses of her imagination,
        as when one dreams
of what one has seen just before falling asleep.
        An outdoor table and umbrella
by the sea with a white sailboat in the distance
and the shadow of the umbrella falling just so,
steeply pitched, across the astonishing pineapple
        and the bottle of wine.
Can a father recover his daughter in a painting?
Or in an orange-and-umber blouse he gave her
        ten years ago?
Well, sometimes the heart in its excess enacts
such pageantry. But it is hollow, hollow.

She died, as she had lived for many years,
        far away.
No doubt my life is more deficient
because I didn't see her expiration. Yet

she could not have known, could not
have twitched her eyelid if I had kissed her
then. The last she said to me, on the phone
      five days before,
was, "Don't grieve for me. That would spoil everything."
As if amidst such spoilage one more tiny ounce
      could make a difference.
Clearly her view of what was happening was
not like mine. My dear, I hope I may
somehow when my turn—soon now—comes
attain your view. But I'm not confident.
An old man is such a frail effigy
in the garden of beautiful young women.

Palinuro was a young man. He was dark
and strong, good-looking, an Assyrian perhaps
      or an African,
a songwriter in his spare time, my friend,
who had been recruited to be the helmsman
on the voyage to Italy, our voyage of conquest.
When the great storm struck, a mountain
of water rose up high beside the ship, towering
in its immensity, shutting out the sky,
and fell across the decks, sweeping Palinuro
overboard. In an instant, an instant, Palinuro
      vanished beneath the waves.

We know his name, yet even that was
probably invented by some poet. What we
      truly know

are death and taxes. These are indubitable.
Martha also had her share of problems in the tax
department. She was a worrier. She schemed
and figured endlessly to pay the vigorish,
which is what she called the health insurance
premiums. Usury on a borrowed life.
Her worries were at least a little distraction
     from her pain.

I'll write a check, a paltry amount but all I
can afford, and send it to my grandchildren.

Martha was married twice, and no man could ask
for better sons to be brought to him by a daughter.
Ames, the musician and entomologist. Then Jerome,
so fittingly named, who cared for her in her illness
selflessly, with abiding affection. Abiding.
Affection was his abode. He is a saint, and who
can imagine now how achingly he is bereft.
Ames too, wherever he is—I think somewhere
in Virginia. This is what we know. This
is everything we know, all that we can share
ultimately. Loss. Loneliness. How appropriate
that knowledge in the bible meant having
sexual intimacy with. The impossible incest.
The illusion of connectedness. Loss in having.

And have we this time reached the culmination?
Martha died in what is called the Age of
Terror—carnage at the airport, bleeding

bodies strewn everywhere, even in the great temple
    at Luxor. This also
is what we know, the continual orgy. The rictus
of death and orgasm. We know that Mother Cosmos
is the greatest terrorist, mailing out letter bombs
every day from her empyrean agency to addresses
    all over the world.

When she was thirteen she had a bathing cap
that made her look, she thought, like a movie star—
a cap made of rubber, close-fitting, white and ribbed. She
wore it all summer. Why not? Even while she was reading
    Catcher in the Rye.

The light is changing. Twilight has come, a peculiar
light, pellucid on the snow even in our
gloomy climate. The apple tree appears to step forward
as if out of Stygian semidarkness, for my greater
approval—the beautiful apple tree. Martha
did not live in a gloomy climate but in the sun,
in a southern place, and when she lay
in her bikini beside the swimming pool
it was as if Phidias himself had placed her there.

A few years later, how scarred she was! The surgeons
left their welts all over her, front and back.
At one time for a year or two they even
planted a pump in her abdomen. Yes, a pump!
A gadget of plastic parts that would direct
chemicals to her liver. She carried it
like a horrible fetus long past the normal

term, but it would not be born. And yet
it moved in her and spoke to her—a whisper—
the child she loathed and feared. Has it been
born now, a dreadful cesarean? My newest
grandchild—a pump? No doubt that's one way
       to look at it.

The first day of Martha's death is over. What
       of the night?

The apple tree is gone. Eurydice has gone back
to hell, weeping and grim, betrayed. The night
is Pluto's cave. I've turned on all the lights
in this little house on the hill, my defiance
of metaphysical reality and the Niagara-Mohawk
Power Corporation. Idly, as so often, I am
staring at my watch, the numbers clicking away,
hours, minutes, seconds, but time is the most
unrealizable quantity. How long has Eurydice
been gone—a moment or always? And now
suddenly the lights go off. Something somewhere
is broken. The autumn wind has blown down
a tree across the lines. Where did I put that candle
I used to have? Somewhere a glitch is glitching, yet
this is a familiar place, I can move in the dark.
Martha was dead for two minutes, then two hours,
then ten, and will it become a day, two days, with her
not here? Impossible. I cannot think of it.
Yet the lighted numbers on my watch keep turning,
ticking and turning. The numbered pages of my books

smolder on my shelves, surrounding me. Alas, my dear,
alas. Time and number are a metaphysical reality
    after all.

Motherhood came to Martha when she was sixteen.
She "fruited early," as I said at the time in a
poem. She came to live with me, a Southern belle
among backwoods Yankees, and she carried it off
beautifully. Enrolled in the local high school,
took her lessons home when they told her
she had become too big and was an embarrassment,
graduated handily, whereupon Ames
graduated from his school too and came north,
and they were married in our house, a moving
little ceremony witnessed by a couple of
neighboring farmers. They went to live in a trailer
on the north side of the settlement. Martha
scarcely made it to the hospital when her time came,
and half an hour later it was all over
and I was a grandfather at the age of forty-eight—
which was not unusual in that region.
The two young people were good parents. This
was the era of the Stones, Joan Baez singing
"We Shall Overcome," the trial of the Chicago
Seven. Martha asked us to baby-sit sometimes
when her class schedule demanded it, and also
occasionally in the evenings when she and Ames
wanted to go out to smoke a little grass and get
mildly tanked. Why not? They and their friends
were in and out of our house continually,

and it was a happy time. But eventually
they moved away to the west to continue their
educations, and our enforced separation—Martha's
and mine—resumed. What is a father who has been
lost in the wreckage of divorce? The first time
Martha saw me (i.e., when she was able to see,
being four years old), she clung to her mother's skirt
and pointed at me and twisted her little body
in a kind of agony and said, "Mama, who is that
young man?" She had been "prepared" for the meeting,
obviously. But what preparation was possible, then
          or ever?

Soon we shall come to the festival of lights that the
          little girl so loved. It must have been
a wonderful festival before the Cathocapitalist Church
destroyed it. He can just dimly remember lighted
          candles on a tree.

Faces fade in and out of his dreams like the lights
across the valley through the shifting bare branches
          of November.

5:00 AM. Peering out into the windy dark.
A confused and windy head, aged and trembling.
Yet the coffee tastes as astounding as ever, delicious
in the morning darkness, the fragrant tobacco smoke
is soothing. I haven't shed a tear. What an awful
heritage this great goddamned American, prairie-Baptist
stoicism is! I blame it on my grandmother's influence—
Ettie from Minnesota, in the eighties of the last

century. But it is everywhere. I would wail and keen,
I would shriek, I would writhe like a Hindu in the street!
    Believe me, it would be a pleasure.

In darkness the numbers on my watch twitch
        in their permutations.
5:14, 5:15—I stare at them. Something mysterious
about these instantly altering forms, something
        mordant and implacable.
Usually I take off my watch at night
        before I sleep, but last night I forgot.

In early, windy light the apple tree
dances wildly, flinging her apples as if
        they were a shawl—
strange apparition of flamenco in
        snowy upstate New York.

Instead, this gush of words, this surging elegy.
From a poet who has been blocked and almost silent
for two years. Yes, the human emotional
mechanism in all its gut-eating horridness
cannot be denied. A release of some dire kind
has been accomplished. How shaming, how
offensive! And like all elegiac words, these swirl
around the question forever unanswered: "What for? What
        is it all for?"

            Born in Chicago, 6 December 1951.
            Parents divorced when she was an
            infant. Lived in Auburn, Alabama,
            with maternal grandparents, then

with mother and stepfather. Public
school. Married first, Ames Herbert;
one son, Britton. Married second,
Jerome Ward; two sons, Hayden and
Robin. AB, Northern Arizona Univ.,
Flagstaff; MA, Arizona State Univ.,
Tempe. Cancer diagnosis, Califor-
nia, 1990. Died, Birmingham, 17
November 1997.

When I remarried—"What?" she laughed. "Again?"—
she took to her new stepmother quickly.
They were the same age. They conducted long
conversations by phone, laughing and teasing,
sweet to my overhearing ears. We were a family
after all. We visited back and forth, as families do,
and spent a vacation together on Cape Cod.
That is, until I became too old and ill to travel.

Sunrise at last, if you can call it that.
     Above the horizon
at the top of the steep eastern hill,
a faint disk has appeared, a dim useless moon
     behind the overcast.

First thing every morning, before I did anything else,
     I used to write to her.
Coffee and cigarettes. I'd sit in the kitchen
in my Morris chair, unsling my laptop, and type
     "Dearest M"—

then I'd spin out anything I could think of that might
distract her for a moment from her pain.
Nonsense, trivia, I used to complain that, alas,
        I am not Marcus Aurelius.
Wisdom for a dying daughter? I had none.
But at least I knew whom I was addressing.
For an hour every morning we were in touch.
I in my old bathrobe, she in her tousled bed,
her brown curls shadowing her smile. For years
she smiled, often she laughed, and the pain-marks
on her lovely face would disappear. When she was told,
back at the beginning, that she had no more than six
months to live, she learned how to live with death
        almost immediately.

Whom am I addressing now? Not Martha. The absence
        is like a hollow in my mind.
Christ, is there no mercy! But of course the concept
        is unnatural.
Her friends then? But I think they care little
        for poetry.
Twenty years ago I'd have made a box,
I'd have planed and sanded, glued the dovetails
neatly, driven the little brass screws of the hinges
with a watchmaker's screwdriver, and chiseled
a sunflower and her initials into the lid. I used to love
        to make boxes.

The telephone is ringing. Somebody wants
to sell him a piece of land in Arizona. He thinks

briefly of the high country around Payson
that he has admired so much, the great forest
of pines. The phone rings again. Already
Martha has been cremated. Already people
are busy making arrangements, establishing
times and places. But he knows he will not
go to the funeral. He could not bear to hear
that mumbo-jumbo intoned over the cold
    ashes of his daughter.

                As a child she was like
                the sapling birch that grew
                at the end of the orchard,
                slim and graceful, fresh
                in the morning light.
                Then she became
                like Diana running naked
                in the woods, standing
                among the deer and hazel
                trees. On her thirtieth
                birthday she was everyone's
                delight, the dream-woman
                of men, the athletic
                and wise preceptor
                of women. And now,
                except in a father's memory,
                she has dispersed
                and gone, so soon,
                so soon.

Noon is the ominous hour. Not midnight
when we celebrate our joy. Not dusk or dawn
when we take our pills and sit back to
consider. Noon is the ominous hour.
The puny sun mounts toward the apogee
and a thin curtain of snow begins to fall.
A father's vision becomes fluttery,
like his breath. He has reached the end
of the first day of his daughter's death. His sight
is hazy as he looks out at the apple tree.

Saturday Morning in Mundane Munnsville

It's true, ignorance was... well, not exactly
bliss, but at least a comfort. I didn't know
that a millennium of complicated literary
history, Chinese and Japanese, poetry, fiction,
and copious theory, came before Bashō.
For years I didn't have to study it.

Saturday Was the First Day of the New Millennium

The risen sun seemed to him like an oyster
    behind the overcast, smiling there. A pale
bloom as remote as Siberia. And how the world
    converts its ordinariness to beauty, he thought,
as he lighted a cigarette and puffed the smoke
    against he window, curling like petals. Why
is it so hard to get rid of time? Now is always
    a moment, an infinitesimal fraction of a
moment, inapperceptible. Yet the oyster smiles
    and the millennium begins, whatever that is.
Already the millennium is beginning to disappear.
    A gray morning, and the windowpane is cold,
and beyond it the soiled old snow is tattering.
    Is it because so soon I am going to die?

Elegance

No elegance is
    ascribed to sweat: dripping from
        the carpenter's nose

onto the clean ply-
    wood. Yet I recall in my
        big sheepskin how I

sweated in the snow,
    heaving the axe and peavey,
        and how sweet it was.

And how jubilee
    cried in jay-song to the gray
        sky, and the white owl

sailed on extended
    wings unerringly among
        the snow-clad spruces.

Letter to Denise

Remember when you put on that wig
From the grab bag and then looked at yourself
In the mirror and laughed, and we laughed together?
It was a transformation, glamorous flowing tresses.
Who knows if you might not have liked to wear
That wig permanently, but of course you
Wouldn't. Remember when you told me how
You meditated, looking at a stone until
You knew the soul of the stone? Inwardly I
Scoffed, being the backwoods pragmatic Yankee
That I was, yet I knew what you meant. I
Called it love. No magic was needed. And we
Loved each other too, not in the way of
Romance but in the way of two poets loving
A stone, and the world that the stone signified.
Remember when we had that argument over
Pee and *piss* in your poem about the bear?
"Bears don't pee, they piss," I said. But you were
Adamant. "My bears pee." And that was that.
Then you moved away, across the continent,
And sometimes for a year I didn't see you.
We phoned and wrote, we kept in touch. And then
You moved again, much farther away, I don't
Know where. No word from you now at all. But
I am faithful, my dear Denise. And I still
Love the stone, and, yes, I know its soul.

The New Quarry

The new quarry in Sheffield has driven my
friends there practically out of their minds.
The noise, the dirt!—my God, in their very
sanctuary where for years they had practiced
their insanities undisturbed. Well, the master
of Zen says, Detach, detach from your possessions!
Especially this little cranny of the planet that you
cherish. Ah, could I tell you, Galway, stories
of the people from Mars who've destroyed the woodland
next to me! Close encounters of the very unpleasant
kind. So let the quarry dust drift down on
your green fields and wonderful fireweed flowers,
just as the ash from Mount Saint Helens whitened
my friend, the lop-eared dachshund of Montana,
making him look more than ever like a
semaphore. The gods in their condominium
up there, Argus and Angus, Mankato and One-Eyed Jack,
are grinning. Let the sons of bitches grin.

New Poems (2001–2005)

Springtime, 1998

Our upstate April
    is cold and gray.
        Nevertheless

yesterday I found
    up in our old
        woods on the littered

ground dogtooth violets
    standing around
        and blooming

wisely. And by the edge
    of the Bo's road at the far
        side of the meadow

where the limestone ledge
    crops out our wild
        cherry trees

were making a great fountain
    of white gossamer.
        Joe-Anne went

and snipped a few small boughs
    and made a beautiful
        arrangement

in the kitchen window
where I sit now
surrounded.

Selected Haiku

My finger held to
the wind, but I felt nothing,
becalmed. This old hill.

*   *   *

One thing is certain.
When Tu Fu got drunk his balls
swung low, just like mine.

*   *   *

She who loved silent
men is tended, while she dies,
by prattling women.

*   *   *

The Japs have haiku,
Afghans ghazals, Greeks epics.
And we have the blues.

*   *   *

By nature haiku
are in nature. Flowers fall.
Bombs burst somewhere else.

*   *   *

The cat and the moth.
Which of them must be wise? One
eats. The other dies.

*   *   *

The flowers of guilt
aren't purple, not quite. They grow
in too dim a light.

*   *   *

The fly. A little
pestiferous pest that comes
back. No matter what.

*   *   *

You can warm your hands
at a candle, but the rest
of you needs loving.

*   *   *

Well, then. October.
The leaves are falling. Haiku
all over the place.

*   *   *

4

Buckthorn. Pin cherry.
Little "weed trees" flourishing
on the fringes. Rain.

*　　　*　　　*

8

You want to learn how?
Think Basie. That treble lilt,
then bass chords mounting.

*　　　*　　　*

13

Far in the pasture
where his sheep grazed the dewdrops
shine briefly at dawn.

*　　　*　　　*

30

"Small cold breezes make
small harmonies." I didn't
say it. Chuang-tzu did.

*　　　*　　　*

32

"Almagenesis" must
mean something, but damned if I
know what. The leaves fall.

Fanfare for the Common Man, No. 2

(Hommage à Aaron Copland)

And here he lies, here at our feet, as usual.
See his black brows still glowering. See
His maggots, his flies. See his tears still
Limpid in his paralyzed eyes. Oh, see, oh,
See how his blood issues slowly on the ground.
And now look up into the strange gray face
Bending to you on the screen, gray and peculiarly
Fractured, crackled and crazed, unidentifiable
As the progeny of any family of man—
Ah, look at the knowledge there of having
Seen this man and then signed the document
Which contrived this death that reverberates
Now in every day and hour across the world.
Let the muted trumpet sound, and let it
Die in the smoky air...

Adoration Is Not Irrelevant

You, my adoration—no fooling—I've
called my auburn-haired beauty
in ignorance, in 70-year ignorance
because that's what people told me—
but you, woman of radiance, shouldn't
I study you more closely. Oh, my love!
Not auburn, then. Perhaps sorrel,
my sorrel-haired beauty, quiet, wild,
hidden in the oaks. Yes, like the 3-year
fallow deer in the far end of the pasture,
exactly. Name me the color, Persephone-
o'-th'-Oneidan-hills, for it is yours too,
tender goddess. Are you here? There? No,
she has vanished to Hades again, in-
constant girl. But my darling is here.
Let it be sorrel, sweetheart, a soothing
yet somewhat exotic color, rare in the
world. I hold you, your breast, your
belly, like new flesh for my own body,
and bury my face in your hair, here
in our mid-autumn kitchen with the
woodstove warming us—well, I am too old,
and you are my young love, you really
are my adoration—let me adore, do
not exclude me in the fashion of fierce
ideological women, let us rather exclude
ourselves in the kitchen with the maple leaves

falling outside, in our comfort, our love
in the altruism of the nearly bodiless,
so pure and yet so powerful, more, more
than our sexes enjoining our fading lust.
Joe-Anne, sorrel-haired, I adore you, I see
and praise your beauty of loving-kindness
beyond every perturbation of the childish
genes and nerves, the glands of our declining
objectivities, my adored woman who loves me
in all the ways of the gentle world and the woods.

Two Poets

Yes, my sweetheart, we sing
The songs of the blacks
With the words of our own tortures
Adapted to theirs,
But their woe, their unappeasable
Disconsolation
Remaining in the rhythms, the falling
From the rhythms, the excruciating
Harmonies. We are hybrids, aliens,
Space creatures, runaways from Uranus,
But our songs, so grave and compelling,
Tell us our thousands
And thousands of years of suffering
And our love.

Navel

Your navel sunk in its softness—
If you were a nautch dancer you'd
Be taken for the concubine
Of the King of Cincinnati—
But, my adoration, you dance only for me
And I alone am aware
Of the mysteries of all your
Parts and fragrances. *All your parts*
And fragrances. O you gauche god
Of this world, consecrate me.
I am the pride and joy of the grass.

On Being Marginalized

That's what the lady said. Said it right
Out, loud and clear. Said, "You've been mar-
Ginalized." Well, thanks. "It's too bad,"
She said. Oh, you bet your frookin' elbow
It's too bad. And what's that I hear behind
My head? Palm fronds creaking? Is this
Friday's footprint? A sad castaway is what
I am, looking everywhere for a bottle, not
The one with a message, but the one with a
Nice drink of cyanide. Here's to you, lady.
So long. May you choke on that martini.

Complaint and Petition

Mr. President: On a clear cold
morning I address you from a remote
margin of your dominion in plain-
style Yankee quatrains because

I don't know your exalted language
of power. I'm thankful for that. This
is a complaint and petition, sent
to you in the long-held right I claim

as a citizen. To recapitulate your
wrong-doings is unnecessary; the topic
is large and prominent and already
occupies the attention of historians

and political scholars, whose findings
will in the near future expose your
incontinent and maniacal ambition
for all to see. Let it suffice to

say that you have warped the law and
flouted the will and wisdom of the
people as no other has before you.
You have behaved precisely as a tin-pot

tyrant in any benighted, inglorious
corner of the earth. And now you are
deviously and corruptly manipulating
events in order to create war.

Let us speak plainly. You wish to
murder millions, as you yourself
have said, to appease your fury. We
oppose such an agenda—we, the people,

artists, artisans, builders, makers,
honest American men and women,
especially the poets, for whom I dare
to speak. We say, desist, resign,

hide yourself in your own shame,
lest otherwise the evil you have
loosed will destroy everything
and love will quit the world.

The Little Girl Who Learned the Saving Way

My little Girl she grew & grew
   —oh the same as you, the same as you—
and became a young woman as beautiful
     as any in the nation.

But personal beauty she would eschew
   —oh the same as you, the same as you—
and made one child & another two
     and took to painting, an honorable

profession. And again she grew & grew
   —oh the same as you, the same as you—
& her painting from its rudimentaries
     evolved in her soul to a wonder,

a wonder. Then in her beauty a cancer grew
   —oh the same as you, my dear, oh the same as you—
She'll make no more babies & only a painting or two,
     & I—Christ I am old, I'm broken & almost through.

How can the father's heart be reconciled
   —or yours, or yours—
to the vanishing of a daughter good & true
     before him into the boneyard? What is ours
in this reprehensible world? And who the hell are you?

Two White Stones

Mimic is as mimic does in the good old land
  of Boston.
 But the light on Beacon Hill has fled
 And Harvard Yard's awash with dead.
 She gets no forwarder at all
 Against the Somerville Shopping Mall.
My love brought me two white stones from the shore
  of Donegal.

Gertie goes where Gertie's gone in the good old land
  of Boston,
 With her rag mop and turned-up toes,
 Her leaky pen, her stuffy nose,
 Surrounded every day at ten
 By wailing kids and crippled men.
But my love brought me two white stones from the shore
  of Donegal.

What the world needs is what they ask in the good old land
  of Boston.
 By the dead of day or the dead of night
 Gertie suspects—and Gertie's right—
 What the world needs is a three-day pass
 And a good swift kick in Gertie's ass.
Yet my love brought me two white stones from the shore
  of Donegal.

The dogs are lean and cats are mean in the good old land
        of Boston.
    What can you give in her hour of need
    To a Washerwoman who's gone to seed
    But a dictionary and an ink-stained dress
    And the "vaunted title" of Poetess?
Oh, my love brought me two white stones from the shore
        of Donegal.

I would not and my love would not in the good old land
        of Boston.
    On Boston Common the lads are sloshed,
    The ladies are large and seldom washed,
    Poetry lies on the ground like sludge,
    Gertie eats money and excretes fudge.
Thank God my love brought me two white stones from the shore
        of Donegal.

        One is for her
        And one is for me,
        Cleansed in the grief
        Of the Irish sea.

February Morning

The old man takes a nap
too soon in the morning.
His coffee cup grows cold.

Outside the snow falls fast.
He'll not go out today.
Others must clear the way

to the car and the shed.
Open upon his lap
lie the poems of Mr. Frost.

Somehow his eyes get lost
in the words and the snow,
somehow they go

backward against the words,
upward among the flakes
to the great silence of air,

the blank abundance there.
Should he take warning?
Mr. Frost went off, they say,

in bitterness and despair.
The old man stirs and wakes,
hearing the hungry birds,

nuthatch, sparrow, and jay,
clamor outside, unfed,
and words stir from his past

like this agitated sorrow
of jay, nuthatch, and sparrow,
classical wrath which takes

no shape now in a song.
He climbs the stairs to bed.
The snow falls all day long.

Small Fundamental Essay

What many people fail to understand
about the art and science of mechanics
is that you may know perfectly what happens
under the hood of your car when you turn on
the ignition, and you may comprehend
to a nicety how the combination of pump
and pressure tank and heating coils produces
hot water when you turn the tap, and yet
the wonder never ceases. That this can be
—and is—is what bestirs the mind and heart.
Ours is a faith that never starts a war
nor rips a living child from its warm womb,
a faith that needs no ghastly hierophant
hung dead upon a cross to speak for us.
It is faith in the miracle of the possible,
faith in the peaceful knowledge of what is true.

                              H.C.
                              December 19, 1997

A Few Dilapidated Arias

1

And thus the morning has descended. Slowly like
a tremulous lady down the great stairs of the East.
What I notice is language pressing in my mind,
surprising me, as in those times when I made poems
like sweet tarts cooling on the windowsill of a
studio in the woods. Day blooms, a somber flower
in our valley, nowhere and now there. Am I
merely misinterpreting some psychic blip?
Or has time changed? Casually the light extends.

2

So let the sentences unfold again, like a measuring rule
jerked into angled shapes that nevertheless trace
the line onward toward resolution. Let them be
a little sonorous, but only a little. And let them,
for my lady's sake—she who evokes this lingering passion
from hoar-faced hebetude—rise up in melopoeia,
plaintively, lovingly, or wonderingly, from time to time.

3

"Liberation" was the shibboleth and slogan
of my time. We even had a magazine by that
name, and now dear Dave Dellinger is dead.

So many have gone with him! And now who is free?
Only our depraved president, who is free to
send thousands and thousands to their slaughter, like calves
tumbling and jumping in the chute at the Chicago
stockyards, where the blood-scent overspreads the city.
And now we've bombed a wedding party in the desert
outside Baghdad! Can you believe it? Bright shreds of
the wedding tent flying away, bloody pieces of people
flying and flopping on the sand. Pieces of the lovely bride,
pieces of the groom, pieces of the attending elders,
pieces of children, musicians, drivers, and the religious
attendants. A bloodbath, truly. The desert wind rises.
The palm trees bow their heads, the desert birds fly
screaming. It is the absolute opposite of an oasis.

4

"Our crumbling civilization"—a phrase I have used often
during recent years, in letters to friends, even in
words for public print. And what does it mean? *Can*
a civilization crumble? At once appears the image
of an old slice of bread, stale and hard, green with mold,
shaped roughly like the northeastern United States, years
old or more, so hard and foul that even my pal Maxie,
the shepherd-husky cross who eats everything, won't
touch it. And it is crumbling, turning literally into
crumbs, as the millions of infinitesimal internal connecting
fibers sever and loosen. The dust trickles and seeps away.

5

Well, old Great-Grandfather Haidie don't know if he's cold
or hot, and dass de truff. Up with the windows! Down with the
thermostat! Oh my. And down with the windows
and up with the thermostat! Yes, yes, old Bess. Give me a
		broiled salmon
and a bottle of bubbly cru, cause we're goin' to be twistin' when
the wagon comes. And you know what kind of wagon I'm talkin'
about! A smooth ride, baby. Hell, you won't even know
you're coasting down the main to the cree-ma-tori-um!

6

"Day by day make it new," said Uncle Ezra, honoring
the ancient master known as Tching. And Ez wrote it
in Chinese on the side of his bathtub, which is where he
liked to do his studying, thus establishing
a precedent for his followers, like K. Rexroth and the
noble Sam of Port Townsend, my beneficent friend.
And indeed on all five of us the sun shone differently
every morning, and on the Emperor Wu too.

7

Now listen up. "Honeysuckle Rose." "Shimmy
Sha Wobble." "Ain't She Sweet." "Four or Five Times."
You hear? They're the silliest songs imaginable. No one
can sing them, no one. And yet... oh, what we did
with them in our great years! It's said that Penelope

wove her beautiful feelings into the worn-out shirts
of the worn-out suitors. It ain't the material, baby,
it's the quality of the imagination. How fortunate
we are to hear Armstrong, Jelly Roll, Omer, et al.,
on these wonderful recordings. Don't you for-
get it! Don't ever forget the soulful "Flat Foot Floogie."

8

The kind and so exquisite French lady who has
translated some of my poems into her language and
her voice has used a phrase that leaps out at me
from the typescript. "Une voix tremblotante," she
says, oh so decisively, so much more expressively
than anything in my mere American. Well, I
could have been born over there too if the gods had
only been paying attention. Fa-la-la, la-la-la, la-la-la.

9

What is the worst part of growing old? you ask.
Ok, my young friends and paltry scholars, I will
tell you. It's becoming incompetent. All my life
I was the epitome of competence; roughly speaking.
I could do anything—cut a hole in a pine plank
with a keyhole saw, for instance, or grind down
the valves of my pickup, or read government manuals,
or teach esthetic philosophy, or… you name it. In
the army sixty years ago I was called "a handy joe,"
which was probably the best compliment I've ever had.

And now? Other people must do everything for me
and for themselves too. I'm useless. Can you imagine it?
I might as well be a common amanita growing
beneath the tall, tall hemlocks in the dark.

10

Nota bene. My generation of Americans
is the last that can tell an ovenbird in the woods
by its little voice. This is a part of our knowledge. This
is a freaking datum. And when we go this knowledge
will go with us. Lost forever. Think of that. Then think
of all knowledge, beginning to end, and of how it will
go, an immense gasp, one of these old rainy days.

11

The guy who meets somebody on the street, offers
his hand, smiles, and says, "You're fine. How am I?"
is not as simpleminded as you might think. "Hi, Doug."

12

"After the malarial onslaughts of style, nevertheless
I returned to myself." Thus the distinguished visitor
from Hungary, Mr Ottó Orbán, as translated by my
pal, Bruce Berlind of the Lake Moraine Road. And
ain't it the truth! We had tons and tons of style—tons,
I say. Does anyone think we were too stupid to be
clever imitators? But the further truth, my dears,

is that we had only a small assortment of commonplace
ideas, from which we made the poetry that astonished
the world and caused the assembled young to utter shrieks
of joy. Was it a brilliant show? Or was it simply
a flop? Ah, now leave me be. I'm returning to myself.

13

Watching the U.S. Open. Watching the spectacu-
larly beautiful Maria Sharapova, her extraordinary
thighs, her seventeen-year-old angelic face, her sweet
breasts glancing when she bends. Fantasizing that I'm
twenty-five with a full head of hair and she has given me
the key to her hotel room—WOW! And then the announcer
says she is six feet tall. Six feet! Coll a p s e... Tell me, You
Geezers of the World, if I can pretend I'm twenty-five
with suave hair and smiling chops why, why can't I
be six-three for ten minutes? I can't. Figure me that.

14

Who loves the motes lost and wandering, spiraling
lazily, or darting with sudden agitation, in the last
ray of sunlight slanting into my woodshed on a Septem-
ber afternoon among the tiered cords of firewood, maple
and ash, that reach above my head—ten cords for my
winter's fuel—loves what the electronic talkers call
reality now, including this old ragamuffin poet who
leans in studious reminiscence here. And I love him.

15

Philharmonia is the country where I live,
the same country where Maestro Ludwig also lived
in 1820, when his deafness was "complete."
My deafness is the sort that comes when I recline
for an afternoon beneath the monumental spruce
of the northern forest, just as it came to me in the womb.
Because all things are music in my genial inmost ear,
and especially all things rendered in our unfailing language,
which is, as we say thankfully, our most abstract
medium, solely of our imagination. And in despite
of our rabble of tenderfoot wistful yearners let me declare
that the music of the heavens is never so grand or splendid
as the music of the earth. Just be still and listen.

16

Yes. Well then, old friend, since you ask, I'll tell you. Go
back ten months, to January, to the VA hospital
in Syracuse where I'm lying on a table, a surgeon
bending over me. She is an attractive and amiable
young woman, of whom I'm already rather fond. (You
know how I am about that.) She is removing a big, dark
cataract from my right eye. Then somehow her hand
slips, and the tiny scalpel damages me, causing
a hemorrhage inside my eye, though I still
don't know exactly what happened—or how. I know
a long time in a codger's life was spent in pain.
And in going back and forth for checkups in the snow.

When I told all this to the guy beside me at the Sportsman's
about a month ago, he said, "Why don't cha sue,
for Chrissake, you'd make a pile off the goddamned feds.
Maybe a million. Maybe five. If I was you
I'd be down to the lawyer's first thing tomorrow
morning. You bet your ass. You could go to old Paul
Noyes over to Sherrill. You know he'll treat you right."
Well, I thought about it. Believe me, I could make good
use of a million or two. And it isn't that I have any more
esteem for the feds than my pal at the bar. But it just seems
that suing would be the Ammurikan thing to do. And who
wants to be a stand-up Ammurikan these days? Not me.
Not I. Not anyone else I know in the whole Northeast.

17

Postscriptum. For now I frequently see in the low part
of my bad eye's field of vision an amorphous white
what-you-may-call-it fleeing leftward and into nowhere,
and each time immediately I think of Alice's rabbit
running across the green croquet field toward its hole.
Tell me, why is this? When I was a kid in the gloam
of Connecticut's dismal crepuscular bed-time I
hated that book more than any other. And I still do.

18

The sound of adolescence was for me no drumbeat
or the warm rhythmic slapping suck I came to know
years later, though somehow I knew even then that

other adolescents, those cruising by in the Model A with
catcalls and laughter, knew it well; no, it was the sound
of wind smacking the lanyard against the hollow flagpole
in the schoolyard next door to the Carruths' house all night
long. A low metallic booming. Vulcan's metronome
counting the hours of my insomniacal anguish. I ask you,
who could even masturbate to that sepulchral bonging?
Nobody, man. Nobody, nobody, nobody—that's who!

19

Species can be exterminated! The words convolved
like sluggish beasts in Darwin's mind while he pounded
his forehead with the thumb of his fist until his pain
reverberated through the night and his tears coursed into
his marshy beard. And we have *lived all our lives* in those
tears which have spoiled our view of Noah's joyful mountain
from our back porch. We have cast our eyes backward and in
for a long time. We have recited dim and dreary verses. Oh how
we have recited! And now the *Times*, the silly old *Times*, has
announced a new species. Yes, by George, and Jesus! Somewhere
in Africa, long ago, creatures much like us, but a lot
smaller, lived and did what they did. Who cares what they did?
They lived. And now their bones live too in their telling us of
their existence. Never say the earth is not extraordinary!
And you, little cousin, yes, you there, the one named Hayden,
reach out your finger, let us touch, ah—you from your
dark, vast, incredible lostness, and I likewise from mine.

20

When I stepped out one morning in crystalline November,
two great turkey buzzards, aka vultures, were circling
over my little hill, above my little woods. Their huge
wings made soundless, intersecting, comfortable circles
against the blue sky and fleecy clouds, very beautiful, very
simple and understandable, yet surprising too, unexpected.
Was something in my woods attracting them, some little
life, suffering, agonized, caught in awful physicality,
hoping to depart? For several years I've been unable
to walk in my woods, semi-hemi-demi invalidated
as I am. It is my greatest loss. And maybe the vultures
were watching me, a little slantwise, where I stood
by my back door, where the sun is gonna shine someday.
Leo, old Boppertop, alas is gone. But he would know.

21

I mind a time, 25 years ago, when I was standing
in my henhouse watching one of my old ladies lay
an egg. Well, she scratched the bedding and turned around four
times, then crouched and pushed, and crouched and pushed again,
and clucked and turned again, and said—so I could understand—
This is one fucking hellova big egg, boss. I sympathized,
but urged her on, with thoughts of a great breakfast bubbling
in my mind. She crouched and pushed again, a good old girl,
until at last she shivered and her comb turned white. An egg
dropped into the nest, and her comb turned red again. It was
a great egg indeed, a "jumbo" at the IGA without a doubt. I

told Geof about it next day, and he looked skeptically at the
sky. Carruth, he said, you're a crock. Worse, you're a projector
of idle fantasies, and he went home to his own henhouse and
watched his young New Hampshire reds lay eggs over
and over. Not one white comb, he said, amongst 'em.
Geof is a real pal, a true-blue from way back. For 25
years he's been kidding me about my hen. It ain't
possible, he says, and he lays it on about crazy old men
who see hens' combs turn white in their woolgathering
afternoons. I believe he even wrote a poem about it,
because he's a first-rate poet too when it comes to
meditating on mundane events. Keep it up, Geof.
Don't stop now. If you do I'll be hurt and disappointed.

22

Say you're the founder and director of a small arts
outfit. Maybe a dance company in Amarillo, or
an experimental theater in Buffalo, or an
avant-garde publisher in Bisbee. You have done
important work. You have a record of excellent
productions. The cognoscenti all agree you are
essential to the cultural health and well-being
of your city, state, nation, and even, many would say,
the world. But you are broke. That's natural. All artists
are almost always broke. You need nontaxable gifts
and grants from the big foundations. But in order to get them
you must be chartered as a corporation-not-for-profit,
and in order to be so chartered you must have a board
of directors. So you appoint a few sympathetic friends

and people who will help to raise subsidies. Then
the gifts come in, you keep working, and in a few years
you are doing better than ever with a significant record
of accomplishment and an enviable reputation. From
time to time new members are appointed to the board.
They become restless and then ambitious, and they begin
to interfere in your working programs. Before you know it,
they begin to organize against you and to conspire
with formerly loyal members of your staff. Dear friend,
this is the end. You have created something so good
that others want it. Before long your retirement is announced;
the coup has succeeded. Is this what we mean when we
speak of the "corporate takeover of America"? It is.
We're corrupted through and through by the capitalist
ethos with its blindness to everything but wealth and power.
We run like frightened mice every whichway, but we have
no place to go. You and tequila are living in Mexico.

23

"Go tell it on the mountain." The wilderness is around
us everywhere, of course, even on Christmas Eve '04,
but not on this mountain, bro. Don't tell anything. We
love the comfort of deer and fox, hemlock and holly, yes,
even the consolation of these lovely mouse-tracks on the
snow. We love our towering beech and maple, as much or
probably more than you love your pile of stones, your
nasty old cathedral. We celebrate the solstice with sap beer
and apple wine. We sing for this special season our hymns
spun from the bear-breath floating out that hole there in the snow.

What cheer could we have more than this as the days lengthen
at last? Pax vobiscum. Give me a little taste of that mincemeat.

24

Next time around, Jean said, meaning in our next
incarnations, your name will be on my dance card.
Here in Rhode Island at Stephen's on a snowy day in
March, this warms my heart, I think literally. Why not?
Sweet Jean, beautiful Jean, Jean of the blonde ringlets
and Celtic eyes, Jean whom I have loved from afar for more
than forty years, Jean of the beautiful poems signed with the
beautiful name, Jean Valentine, my dear, my darling.
Next time around, indeed. Dear Jean, you give me something
to look forward to in that bleak and dark hereafter which
we so disrelish in our happiness here on earth. Oh, Jean,
this is a paper kiss for you. More and warmer will come.
Yay! and Yah! Way to go, Jeannie Baby! I'll see you later.

25

Well, "yes, your metaphysician is a blind man hunting in a
dark room for a black hat, which does not exist." Thus saith
Prince Piotr Kropotkin on his first visit to the U.S. of A.
in 1897 when he dined with the gentility on Beacon Hill
and rapped with the students of Harvard in their rooms. He
spoke of "mutual aid," by which he meant cooperative
economics, and said he favored a federated organization of
society on the American model. He spoke to enthusiastic
audiences in Boston, New York, Chicago, and many smaller

cities, and was saddened by the obvious fact that many
came to see him because he was a prince, not because he
was a political philosopher. He became good friends
with Louis Agassiz and other American naturalists
and scientists, and was himself widely known for his
contributions to the theory of evolution, stressing
the cooperative rather than the competitive behavior
of animal species. He was a benevolent and gentle man,
whom we are pleased to acknowledge as an essential
contributor to the bright and happy heritage of our
American revolutionary thought. Let some other
names be added here in the roster: Johann Most, Ben
Tucker, Burnette Haskell, Al Parsons, Alex Berkman,
Mollie Steimer, Emma Goldman, and of course Nick
Sacco and Bart Vanzetti. Then in our time Paul Goodman,
Noam Chomsky, Denise Levertov, and me and my
friends. And many others, especially in these days
of imperialism in Iraq and the Bush tyranny. When
was it ever more obvious that evil is the State?

26

Month after month in New England and New York this winter
has been overcast, too warm, too wet, with occasional sleet
and not so occasional fog. What a disappointment! We call it
the Gray Winter, and so it will be known, I'm sure,
for many a dismal year to come. We have no snow,
the grass is sere and olive drab, the highway gleams
with water, crusts of ice trip the old woman who goes
out to scatter seeds for the birds. The Gray Winter,

so unprecedentedly hideous. No cleanliness. No
brightness. As old Bill said, the "winter of our discontent."
Otherwise, the beginning of cataclysmic GLOBAL
WARMING. Of this no doubt remains, whatever that stunted
throwback in the White House mumbles on television,
and the outcome is only too easy to imagine. Arrgh!
Remember me in your agony, my children. Think
of what I have foretold. I wrote these words for you.

About the Author

In a career spanning six decades, Hayden Carruth has served poetry in every conceivable capacity. His oeuvre includes forty books of poetry and criticism, a novel, and one of the most celebrated and influential anthologies of the last half of the last century, *The Voice That Is Great Within Us*.

Carruth was a longtime resident of Vermont and now lives in upstate New York, where he taught for many years in the Graduate Creative Writing Program at Syracuse University. Carruth won the 1996 National Book Award for *Scrambled Eggs & Whiskey*, and his *Collected Shorter Poems, 1946–1991* received the 1992 National Book Critics Circle Award and a nomination for the National Book Award. He has been the editor of *Poetry*, poetry editor of *Harper's*, and for twenty-five years an advisory editor of *The Hudson Review*. The Bollingen, Guggenheim, and Lannan Foundations, as well as the National Endowment for the Arts, have awarded fellowships to Carruth, and he has been presented with the Lenore Marshall/*The Nation* Award, the Paterson Poetry Prize, the Vermont Governor's Medal, the Carl Sandburg Award, the Whiting Award, and the Ruth Lily Prize.

This book was designed by Phil Kovacevich. The typeface used for the text is Janson. Although designed by the Hungarian Nicholas Kis in about 1690, the model for Janson Text was mistakenly attributed to the Dutch printer Anton Janson. In the 1930s, Janson Text replaced Caslon as the face of choice for fine bookmaking. Its strong design and clear stroke contrast combine to create text that is both elegant and easy to read.

The Chinese character for poetry is made up of two parts: "word" and "temple." It also serves as pressmark for Copper Canyon Press.

Founded in 1972, Copper Canyon Press remains dedicated to publishing poetry exclusively, from Nobel laureates to new and emerging authors. The Press thrives with the generous patronage of readers, writers, booksellers, librarians, teachers, students, and funders — everyone who shares the conviction that poetry invigorates the language and sharpens our appreciation of the world.

Major funding has been provided by:

Anonymous (2)
The Paul G. Allen Family Foundation
Lannan Foundation
National Endowment for the Arts
Washington State Arts Commission

Copper Canyon Press gratefully
acknowledges Ted Kooser for his
generous Annual Fund support.

For information and catalogs:

COPPER CANYON PRESS
Post Office Box 271
Port Townsend, Washington 98368
360-385-4925
www.coppercanyonpress.org